"In the realm of Christian leadership, the cry for authentic and multiplying leaders has never been more acute. The book before you, penned with a deep understanding of both the gravity and the grace inherent in Christian leadership, stands as a beacon of hope and a clarion call to those called to serve. Josh Komis is the right author to give this insight. He is a local church pastor and a keen thinker who has done his homework. This book promises to be a transformative experience for those who take a deep dive. As you engage with its pages, I hope you will be inspired to embrace your calling with renewed vigor, invest in the lives of those around you, and participate in the unfolding of God's grand vision for leadership within His church.

—Sam Rainer, PhD
President, Church Answers
Lead Pastor, West Bradenton Baptist Church

"If you have a heart to see God do more in and through you, you'll be encouraged and challenged by this book. After a sobering reality check on the current state leadership development, Komis articulates a roadmap for the reader to become a better leader themselves and practical steps to implement with others. This is a great "how to" resource to spur you on in becoming an effective multiplying leader. It's easy to read, engaging, and provides useful steps you can begin to implement immediately."

—Dr. James Peoples
Send Network Florida, Director

"There is an unfolding leadership crisis in American Christianity that, frankly, keeps me up at night. For decades, we outsourced the development of pastors and church planters, but today we scratch our heads wondering where all the leaders went. The urgent need of the hour is for every pastor and every local church to recover leadership development as central to their mission. In *The Multiplying Leader*, Josh Komis provides a timely, thoroughly biblical, well-researched, and unfailing practical guide to leadership development that any pastor or any church can use to re-start the engine of leadership development. Multiplying leaders is the most important work in the world, and this book will show you how to do it."

—Mark Warnock, PhD
Church Planting Residency Director, Family Church
Church Planting Catalyst, Send Network

"A virtuous, spirit-led leader does not measure their success based on the size of their congregation, but by the number of leaders who are born from their following. Leadership is a skill that requires ongoing practice. Komis provides a very clear blueprint towards successfully multiplying leaders and shares a series of great application questions to help the reader apply these learnings. A clarion call has been sounded!"

—David "Bing" Kelly
Nantan Emeritus/Founder of F3 Suncoast
Chief Marketing Office for Gettel Automotive Group

When I heard Josh was writing a book on leadership, my first thought was that he was pretty young to take on such a topic. But it didn't take me long to realize how much time, thought, and attention he has given to how leaders are made. His passion for multiplication combined with exhaustive study has a produced a book that will confront and challenge leaders to take their responsibility to multiply seriously. This book will be a blessing to the leaders who read it and to all the leaders who will be made as a result.

—Dr. Josh Wredberg
Lead Pastor, Redeemer Community Church
Co-Author of *Exalting Jesus in John*

THE MULTIPLYING LEADER

WHY WE FAIL TO EMPOWER THE NEXT
GENERATION OF LEADERS AND WHAT IT WILL
TAKE FOR US TO BRIDGE THE GAP

JOSHUA KOMIS

Copyright © 2024 by Joshua Komis

All rights reserved.

No part of this book may be reproduced in any form or by any electronic or mechanical means, including information storage and retrieval systems, without written permission from the author, except for the use of brief quotations in a book review.

Cover design and interior formatting by *Hannah Linder Designs*
Proofreading and editing by Mary Straits

To my bride and best friend, Lacey. You encourage me to be all that God has called me to be and support me every step of the way. You set a Christlike example for our children and develop them daily to be all that God calls them to be. You are the epitome of a healthy, multiplying leader. I love you.

To my dear children: Titus, Judah, Mercy, and Micah. Your daddy loves you and prays for God to take you farther and bless you deeper than you dare to dream. Follow Jesus and open your sails.

CONTENTS

Foreword	xi
Introduction	xv

1. A MULTIPLYING LEADER'S MOTIVE — 1
Our Spiritual Mandate

God's Design for Christian Leadership	2
Every Man for Himself	4
The Bridge to Eternal Life	5
God–Centered Leadership	8
Our Moment To Invest for Eternity	10

2. OVEREXTENDED LEADERS, EMPTY PULPITS, AND BUSY PROFESSIONALS — 13
The Stark Reality of Christianity Today

Sprinting Not Investing	15
Mile-Wide Bobby	16
Self-Pressured Peter	18
Living in Isolation	21
Failing To Plan	22

3. NEGLECTING THE GREAT COMMISSION — 25
Intentional Discipleship Leads to Multiplication

Microwaving the Faith of the Next Generation	26
Intentional Discipleship	27
Personal Proximity	28
Prioritizing People	30
Propel Pacesetters	33
Application Questions	35

4. REASSESSMENT AND ADAPTATION — 37
Shifting from Burnout to Multiplication

Leading a New Nation	38
A Recipe for Burnout	39
Moses Accepted Help	40
Qualities of an Adapting Leader	41
Looking for Sleeping Leaders	44
Look in the Mirror	46
Healthy, Multiplying Leadership Assessment	48

5. THE MARKS OF A MULTIPLYING LEADER ... 53
   Healthy Leaders Develop Healthy Leaders
   - Spiritually Healthy ... 54
   - Mature in the Faith ... 56
   - Shepherd Leaders ... 58
   - Persistent in Prayer ... 59
   - Trusting Delegators ... 60
   - Application Questions: ... 63

6. THE MARKS OF MULTIPLYING GROUPS ... 65
   Community forms the Soil of Multiplication
   - Alone in Asia ... 65
   - Strong Communities Bear Lasting Fruit ... 67
   - Clear on a Vision To Multiply ... 69
   - Clear on the Need for Gospel Advancement ... 70
   - Relational in Evangelism ... 71
   - Knowledgeable of Their Context ... 73
   - Committed To Minister as a Group ... 74
   - Putting the Pieces Together ... 75
   - Application Questions: ... 76

7. MAKING PROGRESS ... 79
   Practical Steps To Start Multiplying Today
   - The Pathway from Pupil to Mentor ... 80
   - Multiplication at Every Level ... 81
   - Start with One ... 82
   - Small-Group Explosion ... 84
   - Multi-Layered Organization ... 87
   - A Worthwhile Investment ... 90

8. ANSWERING THE CLARION CALL ... 93
   Our Commitment to Moving Forward Together
   - Most Valuable Servants ... 93
   - Sharpening the Axe ... 94
   - Opening the Sails ... 96
   - Leadership Coaching ... 97
   - Outside Consultants ... 99
   - Catalysts for the Kingdom ... 101
   - Ministry is Global ... 101

   Conclusion ... 105
   References ... 109

FOREWORD

In the realm of Christian leadership, the cry for authentic and multiplying leaders has never been more acute. The book before you, penned with a deep understanding of both the gravity and the grace inherent in Christian leadership, stands as a beacon of hope and a clarion call to those called to serve. Josh Komis is the right author to give this insight. He is a local church pastor and a keen thinker who has done his homework. The book is grounded in research while being practical at the same time. Here, he not only clearly diagnoses the leadership void we face but also prescribes a biblically rooted, Christ-centered path forward.

At the heart of this book, Komis provides a compelling examination of the crises confronting Christian leadership today: the burnout of leaders under the heavy yoke of ministry, the departure of leaders from their callings, and the scarcity of leaders ready to step into the gaps left behind. Yet, he does not dwell in the valleys of these challenges. Instead, he helps you understand God's unfailing promises and His eternal plan for leadership—a plan that involves multiplication, spiritual health, and a return to the foundational principles of discipleship as modeled by Jesus Christ Himself.

Komis embarks on a journey through Scripture, history, and contemporary church life to uncover the reasons behind the leadership shortage and its profound impact on the body of Christ. With each chapter, he invites readers to explore how God develops leaders through challenges and triumphs and how we, in turn, can nurture and multiply healthy leadership within our spheres of influence.

What sets this work apart is not merely its timely message but the spirit in which Komis delivers it. The author approaches this critical subject with humility, empathy, and a palpable love for the church and her mission. There is a recognition of the weight of leadership and the toll it can exact, matched by an unshakeable confidence in God's power to renew, restore, and revitalize His people for the work of His Kingdom.

This book is an endorsement of the potential within each Christian leader to effect meaningful, lasting change. It challenges prevailing notions of leadership as a solitary endeavor, highlighting the necessity of community, mentorship, and above all, reliance on the Holy Spirit. Through personal anecdotes, biblical exposition, and practical advice, Komis shepherds readers toward a deeper understanding of their calling and equips them with the tools needed to thrive as leaders who not only show the way but also multiply.

In reading this manuscript, I was struck by Komis's ability to weave theological depth with practical applicability. He imbued each page with a sense of urgency and purpose yet also offers space for reflection, self-examination, and prayerful consideration of one's role in God's redemptive narrative.

This book promises to be a transformative experience for those who take a deep dive. As you engage with its pages, I hope you will be inspired to embrace your calling with renewed vigor, invest in the lives of those around you, and participate in the unfolding of God's grand vision for leadership within His church.

As we stand at the precipice of a leadership crisis, this book not only points us toward the bridge but also encourages us to be the builders of that bridge—bridges that lead to healthy, vibrant, multiplying communities of faith. Let us then, with open hearts and ready hands, respond to the clarion call to arms, to the urgent need for godly leadership, and commit ourselves anew to the task of raising leaders who will carry forward the mission of Christ with faithfulness, courage, and love.

May this book serve as a catalyst for change, a source of encouragement, and a guidepost for all who aspire to lead in the way of Jesus. May we all embrace the challenge to multiply, heal, and lead with the wisdom, grace, and power that comes from above.

> Sam Rainer
> President of Church Answers
> Lead Pastor of West Bradenton Baptist Church

INTRODUCTION
THE LEADERSHIP VOID

This book issues a clarion call.

If you don't know of clarion calls, armies issued them in the Middle Ages around AD 1400. They used a high-pitched trumpet called a "clarion" on the field of battle. Through the disarray, the trumpet call brought clarity and urgency to the soldiers. Later in the 18th century, the clarion call became a proverbial saying for a call to arms or response to an urgent need.

If you serve as a Christian leader in any capacity right now, you likely have heard about a looming crisis. Researchers and practitioners continue to sound the alarm, projecting a shortage of future Christian leaders. Even today, more and more Christians are experiencing empty pulpits, short-staffed ministries, discipling deficits, and/or absent leadership in their families. The world needs more healthy Christian leaders! While many may not understand this need, every Christian leader bears some responsibility to address it.

In this book, I hope to offer clarity on how Christians can become and develop healthy, multiplying leaders in three ways. First, we must uncover reasons for the leadership shortage and its effects on Christian circles today. Second, we must rediscover how God develops people as a key part of his kingdom agenda. Third, we must learn to recognize, develop, and multiply healthy leadership in our spheres of influence.

No matter the scope of your influence, you undoubtedly have people around you whom you can invest in and raise up to lead for Christ. Henry and Richard Blackaby correctly say, "Spiritual leadership is getting people onto God's agenda" (Henry and Richard Blackaby, 2011, 36). Spiritual leaders need to recognize God's full agenda for their leadership and help others to discover God's agenda for them. Before we do that, however, we must look at the current crop of spiritual leadership to see why we need more healthy leaders today.

The Fruit of Our Own Orchard

As I'm writing this, we are entering my wife's favorite season of the year: fall. Down in Florida, our famous oranges and grapefruits are ripe for picking. Up north in Wisconsin, the crisp fall weather is perfect for drinking apple cider and taking home bushels of apples. I have fond memories with my family visiting those orchards and walking among the trees to enjoy the season's bounty. What others so carefully sowed, we so gratefully enjoyed.

Like a crisp apple, good leaders are a gift and meant to refresh others. Tragically, the current state of Christian ministry leaves people with unmet desires and often times, a bad taste in their mouths. Bad fruit means that somewhere along the way, our leadership orchards became infected. I am unable to examine every fruit of unhealthy leadership today, but I will point out several visible signs. We cannot address a crisis without first understanding some symptoms. Furthermore, our own personal habits and decisions (or lack thereof) are possibly contributing to this problem. If so, we cannot continue to lead the same way and expect different results.

Burned Out Leaders

One major factor in our leadership crisis, ministerial burnout and fatigue, continues to increase. In 2022, Barna Research Group examined data trends on church leaders between 2015 and 2022. Many of these Christian leaders reported a significant decrease in their overall well-being, joy, and confidence in their calling (Barna Group, 2022). Sadly, others struggled to maintain not only their joy but also their physical health in their service to Christ. Barna CEO David Kinnaman later told Carey Nieuwhof, "A drop in the level of pastoral health this significant in just seven years isn't just unprecedented, it signals a crisis that the church has to address" (Nieuwhof, 2023).

Furthermore, when ministers burn out, their families hurt as well. Almost half of pastors and their wives say that they have experienced burnout or depression to the point of taking leave from ministry (Ash, 2016, 16–25). Clearly, Christian leadership is in crisis. We can no longer ignore the volume of hurting pastors or assume that doing ministry the same way will yield different results.

At one time experts estimated a staggering 1500 individuals left pastoral ministry each month due to burnout (Barna, 2014). One-third of those pastors claimed to experience burnout in their first *five* years of ministry. That means that if one of these pastors went through a traditional three-to-four-year Master of Divinity program, he burned out or quit in nearly the same amount of time.

Unfortunately, we didn't take enough steps to address the problems revealed in 2014, and nothing will change in 2024 if we don't take the problem seriously and take decisive action.

First, we cannot multiply healthy leaders without spiritually healthy leaders to begin with. Of course, the global impact of COVID-19 has put significant pressure on Christian leaders. Intensifying workloads, decision fatigue, and heavier emotional burdens have certainly played a role in wearing down leaders. However, the trends of burnout existed before the pandemic, which only intensified the demands on leaders. Today's Christian leaders face heavier emotional burdens and responsibilities and spend more time putting out proverbial fires. While many factors contribute to burnout, fighting such fires alone accelerates burnout.

In his insightful book *Zeal without Burnout,* author Christopher Ash shares correspondence with a friend about ministry leadership and firefighting. This unnamed firefighter friend described how firefighters cannot battle a blaze alone: "It's foolishness to ignore your limitations, try to be the hero, and cramp up, pass out, or have a heart attack...because you're beyond the limits of what God has supplied you with the capability of doing" (Ash, 2016, 16–25). He goes on to say, "It's a form of heroic suicide and is counterproductive because now you're no longer effective in fighting fire and the resources that were dedicated to fighting the fire are now dedicated to you" (Ash, 2016). Ash makes a clear parallel between firefighting and leadership burnout.

As the missionary and apostle Paul clearly testifies, a servant of King Jesus fights many fires and bears many burdens (2 Cor 11:23–29). Spiritual warfare is real, and people continually need help getting back onto God's agenda. Paul fought many fires including, but not limited to, doctrinal heresy, disgruntled churches, persecution, unrepentant sinners, false apostles, personal attacks, and daily anxieties. Paul's orientation to Christianity began with the risen Lord saying, "I will show him how much he must suffer for the sake of my name" (Acts 9:16). In short, Paul faced roaring wildfires in his spiritual journey and ministry. By God's grace, he fought those fires and finished his race well (2 Tim 4:7). By no coincidence, he also intentionally invested his life and multiplied healthy spiritual leaders, including Timothy and Titus. He shows today's leaders that they, too, can face tests in leadership, make time for people development, not burn out, and finish their races well.

At the same time, ministering to others in Jesus's name is not an easy assignment and requires hard work and sacrifice. God, however, did not design leadership to destroy us. By the power of his Spirit and his vast supply of grace, we can go the distance. We cannot, however, go the distance alone. In fact, many leaders are experiencing burnout because too many firefighters have attempted to work solo. We fail to raise up and empower other leaders to help serve with us on the front lines. The fire will inevitably claim more victims, including ourselves, without strategic action.

Departing Leaders

Aside from burnout, a tidal wave of church leaders will soon leave their positions for a variety of other reasons ranging from emotional hardships, to stress, to retirement. Again, loneliness plays a major factor in this impending great departure. In March 2022, Lifeway Research reported that 42% of pastors surveyed were seriously considering quitting the ministry altogether. The top two reasons they listed included "the immense stress of the job" and "loneliness and isolation" (Lifeway Research, 2022). An increased departure in Christian leaders will cause a ripple effect in those who pick up the slack (Rainer, 2022).

While noting the shortage of Christian leaders overall, Rainer says, "One of the most common challenges we hear from church leaders, particularly pastors, is the need for more leaders in the church. The vacuum seems the greatest among elders, deacons, and teachers" (Rainer, 2023). At a time when we need more help, many pastors will retire in the next decade. David Roach, from Christianity Today, estimates about 25% of pastors plan to retire in the next seven years and many fear they will not have a successor ready to take their place (Roach, 2023).

Because leadership requires presence, unless we have experienced, healthy leaders present, they cannot replicate. Some of these pastors are willing to plan for succession but don't know where to look. If we fail to heed these warning signs of our impending leadership shortage, we will experience catastrophic consequences. At this rate, thousands of churches will have empty pulpits. The leaders who remain will likely struggle under the additional burden of responsibilities. Worse, ministries will turn to ill-equipped or spiritually unhealthy practitioners.

Spiritually Unhealthy Leaders

Notably, Christian leaders find themselves in headlines all over the world. Unfortunately, these headlines stand out for the wrong reason, causing public distrust of Christian leaders to surge. *The Houston Chronicle* published a stunning report in 2019 on hundreds of cases of sexual abuse within the Southern Baptist Convention. In many of those cases dating back twenty years, churches ignored or covered up the abuse, or predators simply resigned, and another church later rehired them (Downen, Olsen, and Tedesco, 2019). A president of the largest evangelical seminary in the world made headlines for his resignation due to ungodly behavior and scandalous marital issues. In 2021, *Christianity Today* released a podcast called *The Rise and Fall of Mars Hill*, which details the excesses and problems with Pastor Mark Driscoll and the staff culture at Mars Hill Church in Seattle. It skyrocketed to number one on Apple's religion podcasts and has over 2.5 million downloads.

Social media feeds fill with similar narratives of church hurt and abusive charismatic leaders (Wax, 2021). Streaming services fed on this phenomenon and released exposes like *Shiny, Happy People: Duggar Family Secrets* on Prime Video. Hulu released its own documentaries called *The Secrets of Hillsong* and *God Forbid*. Clearly, the "rise and fall" of Christian leaders captures modern interest and hinders the trust of both believers and unbelievers around the world.

As a result, unhealthy spiritual leaders have made a large impact on the world. The public's perception of Christian leaders is at an all-time low (Brenan, 2023; Earls, 2023). Christ calls his church to shine brightly as ambassadors for him (Matt 5:13–14) but some of our leaders seem to bear a closer resemblance to the prince of this world.

I'm crying as I write these words. This issue is personal for me. I have friends and former classmates who made a shipwreck of their calling. I know families torn apart by sin and spiritually destructive habits. I know leaders who burned out after battling alone. I personally have failed at times to fully grasp God's vision for multiplying spiritual leaders. Ecclesiastes 3:4 tells us that "there is a time to weep." Brothers and sisters, now is the time to weep. We must stop shooting ourselves in the foot and the next generation in the heart. We need a change in the climate of Christian leadership and a call back to God's purpose.

Hope for Change

After acknowledging the considerable gap in healthy leadership, we can repent and start following God's way. Without a powerful move of God, we will not see revival in Christian leaders. All our efforts to multiply leaders will fall short. We need to become humble leaders centered on God's Word and lead by his strength and for his glory. As we do, we will become spiritually healthy leaders who can carry out God's blueprint for Christian leadership. We will see a movement of multiplication.

Thankfully, I'm encouraged that more and more leaders recognize their need for help. Many leaders recognize their need and realize they must do something new to raise up a new generation of leaders. Despite our brokenness, we long for something better. We want to recover God's plan for leadership. God graciously grows his seed in the soil of humility.

Jesus loves working with our meager offerings. Before he fed the 5,000, he instructed his disciples that they should feed the people (Matt 14:16–18). They lamented that the only food they possessed was a little boy's lunch. Jesus said, "Bring them here to me." He took the single lunch and turned it into a feast for thousands. He could have created the feast all on his own. Instead, he used this as a teaching moment to help the disciples see a very important truth. Apart from him, we can do nothing. He is the bread of life and the multiplier. He brings health, sustenance, and abundant provision. He can work through our meager offerings and multiply fruit to the benefit of many. As the ultimate multiplying leader, he shows us how to do the same in our ministries as we walk with him.

We don't just need loads of leaders or more talented people. We need leaders hungry for Jesus, his kingdom, and his will. God can use one imperfect leader to make an incredible difference in the world. Since you're reading this work, I assume you desire to become one of those leaders. I sincerely hope that this book can serve as a clarion call and guide for you.

Take the first step to lasting change with awareness and self-reflection. If you have been leading for years, are you willing to reassess the blind spots in your leadership practices? If you are new to leadership, will you accept the mantle to help multiply healthy leaders?

With this book, I desire to help new and experienced Christian leaders alike take clear steps to healthier, multiplying leadership. In the coming pages, we will rediscover God's beautiful plan for spiritual leadership and why multiplication matters. We will confront some of the reasons we fail to multiply. We will study the ways of King Jesus and how he invested his time and life into his disciples. I will also share successful practices of healthy multiplying leaders and groups today. As a result of this journey, you will be able to take practical steps to replicate healthy spiritual leaders in your ministry.

Ultimately, the God of heaven who created us to know and glorify him to the fullest of our God-given capabilities has called us to do so. By his grace, we can see a future where many healthy leaders serve Christ joyfully and raise up the next generation of leaders. The future is bright. Respond to the clarion call!

1

A MULTIPLYING LEADER'S MOTIVE
OUR SPIRITUAL MANDATE

"For by him all things were created, in heaven and on earth, visible and invisible, whether thrones or dominions or rulers or authorities—all things were created through him and for him." Col. 1:16

In the San Gabriel Mountains of Southern California lies a peculiar arch bridge. The well-constructed bridge stands 120 feet tall over the middle of the river canyon. Built in 1936, the original design called for the bridge to continue the East Fork Road between the San Gabriel Valley and Wrightwood, California. Unfortunately, a great flood in 1938 washed out most of the road, ending the project. Today, the bridge still stands, but practically speaking, it serves no purpose. Only hikers can access this bridge and only hikers who commit to a challenging 10-mile round trip. People today know the structure only as "The Bridge to Nowhere."

Christian leadership works like a bridge but not a bridge to nowhere. Effective spiritual leaders guide people from where they are to where God wants them. God did not create leadership for the glory of leaders or leadership but for his glory and the benefit of others. Furthermore, God wants to use his people to their maximum potential, and true spiritual leaders will do the same. Leaders who lose track of the needs of their people or God's vision for leadership may look like good leaders externally but will not fulfill their original purpose, just like the Bridge to Nowhere.

Numbers of dynamic leaders in society today excel at raising funds, managing organizations, or influencing work groups, but they fail as bridge builders for the next generation. If we leaders neglect to help our people maximize their gifts according to God's plan for their lives, we have missed an opportunity to be an effective bridge.

The current shortage of healthy, multiplying leaders points to confusion over a vital purpose of leadership: replication. We cannot have confusion here because leadership matters too much. We need more leaders to embrace God's blueprint for Christian leadership and multiply other leaders who will do the same.

God's Design for Christian Leadership

As early as the first chapter of Genesis, God reveals the essence of healthy leadership. God designed men and women as spiritual leaders with a clear purpose: to glorify God and to help people discover his fullest potential for them.

In the beginning, God made all things (Gen 1:1). Like a master painter, he created towering trees, starry skies, diverse animals, and breathtaking sunsets. All of these elements shouted his glory, but on the sixth day, God created his greatest masterpiece yet. He created man and woman in his image. They had immense value and dignity because they reflected God's likeness in their existence, but God also gave them a mission: "'Be fruitful and multiply and fill the earth and subdue it and have dominion over the fish of the sea and over the birds of the heavens and over every living thing that moves on the earth'" (Gen 1:28).

A mighty, eternal, relational, and gracious Creator, God created us to know him and chose us as his personal representatives to share his leadership over earthly creation. We have the unique standing as humans to represent the glory of God and to spread his glory throughout the world. God promised to bless humanity as they obeyed his revealed will.

He also promised to bless them with the ability to multiply image bearers for him. He said, "it is not good for man to be alone" (Gen 2:18) and created woman to help man cultivate the earth. God told them to enjoy a fruitful marriage and multiply offspring over the earth. By having children also made in the image of God, Adam and Eve experienced a previously untapped joy: they could help replicate image-bearers for God.

Multiplication advanced the promises and blessings of God. Kenneth Mathews explains in his commentary on Genesis how "Adam fathered a 'son' in his own 'likeness' and 'image' (Gen 5:3), which showed that the Adamic family continued the imago Dei and the divine blessing first received by Adam (Gen 5:3–31)" (Mathews, 1996, 169). God designed Adam's line to extend more fully to reflect God's glory. Just as God designed the first man and woman to represent him and participate in his work, every new human could fully participate in that kingdom work as well.

Parents would raise their offspring, full of untapped potential, to also join God in his long-term goal to cultivate the earth. Imagine the joy of seeing your children, who look like you but even more like their God, learn to build, explore, design, help others, and serve alongside you. You would not hinder their development; you would cheer them on! You'd give them all the knowledge and resources you could. Together, the entire first family and ensuing generations would continue to reflect God's design in identity and mission.

Developing the next generation would take an incredible amount of time and energy. Yet, if Adam and Eve obeyed God, development would not exhaust them. They would produce offspring who would multiply God's blessings in their lives, share the burden of their mandated responsibilities, and reflect God's glory to the ends of the earth. The Bible shows from the beginning that a proper view of Christian leadership, parenting or otherwise, must involve healthy multiplication for God's kingdom and glory.

So what happened to this beautiful blueprint?

Every Man for Himself

Tragically, Adam and Eve disobeyed God and rebelled against his commands. He told them not to eat of the Tree of the Knowledge of Good and Evil (Gen 3:15-17). When the serpent tempted her, Eve began to question God's word and goodness. Adam, instead of leading his wife to resist those lies, stood silently nearby, a clear abdication of spiritual leadership (Gen 3:6). Man and woman rejected God's calling and ate the fruit.

Sin marred their identities and corrupted their calling. Instead of revealing God's glory to the world, they dragged creation into the depths of darkness with them. When God confronted Adam about his sin, Adam blamed the woman for his personal disobedience. Eve could no longer count on Adam to glorify God or serve her best interests. Taken aback, Eve also deflected her personal responsibility and blamed the serpent. In an ironic twist, they claimed no dominion over the earth and acted subservient to creation. From then on, people began to live for themselves and their selfish ambitions. They lost the blueprint to live and lead for the glory of God.

Sin opened an eternal gap between our glorious Creator and humanity and brought devastating consequences on the family unit and the world. The first son of man, for example, murdered his brother. The stain of original sin continues to multiply brokenness on the earth and leads people to an eternal punishment apart from God (Rom 6:23; Mark 9:42–48). Like the Bridge to Nowhere, sin severed humanity's spiritual relationship to God.

The Bridge to Eternal Life

Humanity stood on the edge of a precipice without any desire or hope of restoring their relationship to God. They could not build a bridge to get to God or love others. In an act of incredible grace, God chose to reach out to man (1 John 4:19). Completely holy and loving, he pursued the full redemption and restoration of his people. He was determined that his glory would shine, and he would lead his people from spiritual slavery to eternal freedom.

Even though people utterly wrecked their relationship with God, the God of all grace made a way. Isaiah 43:16 and 19 says, "Thus says the LORD, who makes a way in the sea, a path in the mighty waters, Behold, I am doing a new thing; now it springs forth, do you not perceive it? I will make a way in the wilderness and rivers in the desert."

To fulfill God's promises and redemptive plan, God the Son stepped down into this world, took on human flesh, lived the perfect life, took our sins upon himself on the cross, and shed his blood to atone for the sins of the world. Three days later, God raised him from the dead. His empty grave opens the door to all who repent and believe in him to have eternal life with God. Jesus, the ultimate multiplying leader, is the bridge to eternal life.

The gospel is the good news that Jesus came to redeem us from sin and to free us to live out God's design. Paul tells us, "For we are his workmanship, created in Christ Jesus for good works, which God prepared beforehand, that we should walk in them" (Eph 2:10). God did not let the corruption of this world keep his people from fulfilling their part in his grand design. By faith, his sons and daughters represent him on earth (2 Cor 5:20) and shine his glory to the nations (Matt 5:16).

Paul explains the miraculous transformation of our hearts and how God reclaims his people for glory: "But God, being rich in mercy, because of the great love with which he loved us. Even when we were dead in our trespasses, made us alive together with Christ—by grace you have been saved— and raised us up with him and seated us with him in the heavenly places in Christ Jesus" (Eph 2:4–6).

I can never get over what Jesus has done for me. He saved me from the depths of sin and darkness. He delivered me from the depths of Hell and brought me into his family! Because of his sacrifice, I know the Father. He also chose to plant his Spirit within me and use me for his redeeming purposes throughout the world. We have this kind of Redeemer King. Jesus raises people up. He gives us an inheritance and place in his kingdom. His new creation work begins in the heart, mind, and hands of his people. He has created us for glory and will settle for nothing less than using us for his fullest purposes to the end of the earth.

Jesus told his disciples a seemingly impossible word. "Truly, truly, I say to you, whoever believes in me will also do the works that I do; and greater works than these will he do, because I am going to the Father" (John 14:12). This promise seems impossible! The lowly apostles could not miraculously feed thousands more than Jesus did on the hillsides of Galilee or perform a greater miracle than Jesus's resurrection from the dead.

D.A. Carson explains the meaning of the promise writing "that the very basis for their greater works is his [Jesus] going to the Father" (Carson, 1991, 496). In a beautiful heavenly moment, Jesus ascended to the Father's right hand and opened the gates of heaven wide for his people (Heb 1:3; Luke 22:69). From his throne in heaven, the Lord Jesus sent his Holy Spirit to fill, empower, and direct his church. Jesus told his inner circle, "But you will receive power when the Holy Spirit has come upon you, and you will be my witnesses in Jerusalem and in all Judea and Samaria, and to the end of the earth" (Acts 1:8). Never before did people experience the presence of God so close and personal or have the ability to do God's will from the heart, with God's power.

Jesus did not leave his disciples leftovers in the kingdom. He rescued these young men, called them, and equipped them for the calling of a lifetime. The "greater works than these" means that all who have faith in Jesus will enjoy this fruitful calling. This promise applies to "all believers, not just the apostles" to enjoy these blessings (Carson, 1991, 496). Christ builds his kingdom through his people, and one day we will reign with him in his kingdom (2 Tim 2:12; Rev 2:25–26; Rev 20:4; 1 Cor 6:1–3). We will bask in the light of his grace, all of us undeserving but useful for his good purposes.

We can do nothing less than stand in awe and worship our patient, wise, and loving triune God. No one else would desire to heal such a broken people and restore us to be his image bearers for all eternity and exercise spiritual leadership in his kingdom. We exist for his glory alone! We dare to hope that God could use us this way, not because we are deserving, but because he promises that he will. Though we may feel like bumbling disciples, the King of Glory will glorify himself through us. He desires to fill his people with the Spirit to the ends of the earth. Christ, our bridge to eternal life, is at the center of it all, but God chooses to work through his people to guide others along life's path to fulfill his plan and purposes.

God–Centered Leadership

God-centered leaders can never get past their awe of Christ. They enjoy the abiding presence of King Jesus, who transforms them. His or her personal awe and worship of God fuels everything else and impacts others. A truly God-centered leader desires others to see and experience the fullness of Christ. A God-centered leader knows they do not need any leader more than they need Christ. In the vein of John the Baptist, such leaders say, "He must increase, but I must decrease" (John 3:30).

As well-known church leaders Eric Geiger and Kevin Peck say, "God-centered leadership is rightly employed when it aims to fill the whole earth with other renewed image bearers by spreading the gospel and multiplying children of God" (Geiger and Peck, 2016, 64).

We cannot improve on God's original design, but the gospel allows us to recover and maximize it!

Mark Liederbach echoes this heartbeat in *Chasing Infinity: The Pursuit of Infinite Treasure*: "God created humans for this purpose. From start to finish the Scriptures bear witness to His desire to teach us how to maximize that for which He created us" (Liederbach, 2019, 10). God's primary purpose for you is to know, love, become like, and glorify Christ. I hope you see this gospel potential that lies within your innermost being. God makes no mistakes, and he created you for a purpose.

The universal Great Commission of Christ calls for believers to prioritize making disciples for his glory and the maximum good of others. As such, we cannot isolate Christian discipleship from leadership. As we yield ourselves to the Spirit of Christ, we bear fruit of his working on our lives (Gal 5:22–23). His love, joy, and peace reign and multiply in our being. As we grow in maturity and spiritual health, we should desire for those blessings to multiply in the lives of others. God wants others to experience the same hope and uses us to build bridges to guide them to a fruitful life.

To be sure, non-Christian leaders can help people too. Even without an accurate view of God's blueprint, they can create helpful organizations, improve lives, and advance benefits for the common good. The image of God imprinted on our hearts reverberates even through the fracturing of sin. You do not have to be a Christian to be a good doctor, mechanic, CEO, or social worker. If you are one of those helpful leaders, I want to thank you.

Christian leadership differs in that we personally know the One for whom all things exist and his plan for our lives. We can walk in his ways and help seek the fullest good for others. The gospel is the good news for all people in all times and in every situation. Once you experience the gospel of God yourself and know his blueprint for life, you will better know how to help others cross bridges to a fruitful life in Christ.

When we see people the way that God does, we see enormous potential. God will soften our hearts so that people turn from objects or organizational cogs to valuable partners. Like Christ, we should want others to "do greater works" because he is on the throne.

J. Oswald Sanders said that a spiritual leader must be willing to trust others and "devote time to training younger men to succeed and perhaps even supersede him" (Sanders, 1989, 179). We pursue the fullest possible development of spiritual power and fruit by investing in the lives and calling of the people in our sphere of influence. In fact, if Christ is our center and motivation, then we can sincerely desire that they lead a more fruitful ministry than we do (Rom 9:3).

We should value every person in our organizations as if they were the greatest leader of the next generation! God gave you influence to raise up the next generation of servant leaders. Use it wisely.

Our Moment To Invest for Eternity

God has given us life to make an eternal impact. He also gives us unique giftings and abilities to advance his redeeming work. We serve at his pleasure. Instead of drawing attention to the prowess of the individuals, the Bible uses the term "servant" far more often than "leader." God used men and women of all varieties throughout the pages of his story: prophets, priests, kings, judges, parents, couples, singles, businesspeople, and government officials.

Perhaps no one better illustrates this servant leadership than John the Baptist. He proclaimed, "He [Jesus] must increase, I must decrease" (John 3:30). John's ministry gave way to Jesus and the disciples. A young man in his 30s, the swing of a sword in a prison cell ended John's earthly ministry. He did not cling to his life or ministry because he understood his ultimate purpose. He existed to proclaim the glory of God and help the people of Israel prepare for the Savior.

Something endured beyond John's death: his disciples. In the scene unfolding in John 1:35–37, John the Baptist saw Jesus and told his disciples, "Behold the Lamb of God!" At this point, John's disciples began to follow Jesus. John focused on God's plan and gave his disciples permission to pursue God's highest calling. John understood the times and maximized his life to point others to the King.

We want to use our time in leadership like John so that the impact echoes for eternity. John Maxwell challenges us that "too often leaders put their energy into organizations, buildings, systems or other lifeless objects. But only people live on after we are gone. Everything else is just temporary" (Maxwell, 2007, 260). We don't want to waste a minute of this life building bridges to nowhere. We need to rediscover God's blueprint for healthy, multiplying leadership and guide people to their fullest potential in Christ.

We replicate so that we can pass the torch of God-centered leadership to the next generation. Imagine the impact that one healthy, multiplying leader can make for future generations. Make no mistake, God placed you at this point in human history to spread his kingdom work. Are you investing your time in building the next generation of healthy leaders? Most leaders in the Western world are not. Let's turn to see some of the common reasons for this neglect.

2

OVEREXTENDED LEADERS, EMPTY PULPITS, AND BUSY PROFESSIONALS

THE STARK REALITY OF CHRISTIANITY TODAY

Multiplication signifies health. Healthy cells multiply into growing children. Healthy businesses multiply with new locations, employees, and innovations. Healthy churches multiply other healthy churches. Healthy Christian disciples multiply healthy Christian disciples.

In line with this design, God calls Christian leaders to develop Christian leaders. If we Christian leaders are honest with ourselves, however, we're not effectively developing leaders. Whether due to peer pressure, neglect, or misaligned priorities, we are part of the problem, and our failure to multiply healthy leaders indicates that we need a spiritual realignment.

While serving as a reading professor for my doctoral project, Keith Whitfield posed this insightful question: "If leaders or groups are not multiplying, could they truly be classified as healthy?" He recognized the connection between spiritual health and multiplication that all too many Christians miss: healthy disciples make disciples; healthy leaders develop leaders.

Brandon Crawford, an Independent Baptist leader, reported a shocking conversation with seminary staff. He was attempting to help a small church near his find a pastor after three years without one. He logically called a local seminary for prospects. The seminary did not have a single name to share with him. Furthermore, the seminary informed Crawford of "a 35:1 ratio right now of empty pulpits to available pastoral candidates" (Crawford, Baptist Bulletin, 2022). Crawford reports that out of 2,000 Independent Baptist chaplains, ministers, and camp directors, nearly 40% are 60 or older. Churches used to be able to look to the seminaries for new crops of pastors and leaders, but Crawford's experience issues a warning for the American church.

We can't look at this barren crop and blame someone else. We're laborers in this field together and can't look elsewhere for quality leaders any longer. We must evaluate our ministries, understand God's call, and pursue multiplication within our own congregations.

I recognize that the need for Christian leaders goes far deeper than just the senior pastor role. Still, I find these vacancies particularly significant. When the local church lacks a vision for multiplying healthy leaders, the believers in that flock will struggle to pick up the slack. I do not pretend to know all the reasons why you struggle to multiply leaders in your organization. I cannot prescribe a one-size-fits-all solution. While leadership coaching can help you navigate such obstacles, no book, coach, or conference can change the way that you lead. You must be willing to look in the mirror for signs of unhealth and initiate change. Most of us have unintentionally placed God's vision for multiplication in the backseat as we engage in our weekly sprint.

Sprinting Not Investing

If there are Christian leaders on this earth who do not consider themselves busy, I have yet to meet them. Leaders face increasing demands on their time and schedules. They take time to evaluate and make decisions in an increasingly complex world. Some constantly sit in meetings and respond to email and phone calls. Adapting to the frantic pace, we Christian leaders can easily overextend ourselves. Overextension looks like taking on more responsibilities without delegating any of our prior workload. Ignoring the warning signs, leaders begin to work inhuman hours and cut back on rest. When leaders overextend themselves, they can damage themselves, their loved ones, and ultimately, the ministry for which they overextended themselves in the first place.

In a healthy and growing family, dad and mom expend tremendous amounts of energy to nourish their children. When the children are infants, the parents change many diapers, draw baths, and spoon feed them. As the children grow, the parents will need to devote more time to training the children to take care of themselves. Children need to become potty trained and be able to feed themselves. Parents cannot continue to perform these functions for their children and at the same time help them with a task like completing homework. One day, these children will need to learn how to make complex decisions like driving a car on the road and paying for insurance. Eventually, they should be able to move out of the house and function as a full-fledged adult. If the weekly sprint becomes the reason that we fail to develop, our children remain in diapers, and we've missed the goal of parenting.

Overextended leaders appear to accomplish many things on the surface, but they rarely slow down to invest in the next generation of leaders. They are stretched too thin and have too little time in their schedules to sit down with new leaders and offer deep guidance. We're not helping our ministry members grow in maturity. We must break the cycle. We cannot allow busyness to eclipse our work in raising up the next generation of leaders. God never calls us to sacrifice his plan for the tyranny of the urgent. A hurried leader who does not take time to develop leaders exasperates his or her own long-term challenges. We might be able to justify this neglect in the short term, but anyone who fails to raise up leaders in the long term, will feel the strain even more.

I'd like to share some real-life examples where leadership overextension negatively impacted others. We must listen to their stories and recognize our own propensity to replace healthy ministry with hurry.

Mile-Wide Bobby

Pastor Bobby has served for decades at his church in South Carolina. Under his leadership, the church grew steadily. Now, this growing church demands more of his time, and his people lean heavily on his presence and attention. A single pastor, he happily obliges and dedicates most of his time to his church community. He tries do it all and typically does, at least superficially. The church expects him to preach every Sunday, teach Bible studies, visit the shut-ins, and attend community functions.

Unfortunately, as Bobby stretches wider, he does not often maintain the same spiritual depth. His personal worship and prayer times with Jesus become shorter and more sporadic. Often, he spends his only Bible reading for the day preparing for the next message or chaplain visit. His personal walk with Jesus suffers because he lacks accountability and discipleship. Bobby's pace also precludes him from taking care of his body and exercising.

With all he has going on, Bobby certainly does not slow down to invest in emerging leaders. He has a young assistant pastor named Ted who tries to learn from Bobby, but Bobby brushes him off. He can spare only about ten minutes with Ted in the church parking lot before Bobby speeds off to his next appointment. Bobby "delegates" attending committee meetings to Ted, which Bobby was not planning to attend anyways. Helping others through a decision-making process is not the best use of his time, or so he thinks.

Pastor Bobby is a nice guy who loves the Lord and cares about his church. As we observe Bobby's leadership in action, we must recognize symptoms of unhealth. For starters, Bobby is not accepting his God-given limitations.

Healthy, multiplying leaders recognize their limitations. God created humanity with natural limits as a gift of his grace, not as a curse from sin. Though God has no physical limits, he chose to rest on the seventh day of creation (Gen 2:2–3). He called the day holy and a blessing. "So God blessed the seventh day and made it holy, because on it God rested from all his work that he had done in creation" (Gen 2:3). If our Creator chooses to rest for his glory and to enjoy his creation, we dependent creatures must not exceed our limits. We cannot function well without good amounts of sleep. We cannot be fully present in multiple places at once even if technology tricks us into thinking we can. We cannot create more hours in a week. Healthy leadership recognizes that our God does not need rest or have time constraints, but we finite creatures certainly do.

Jesus, the Son of God, was also fully human. When God the Son took on human flesh, he physically limited himself to operate the same way as every other human. Mark records an interesting juxtaposition. The locals craved more time with Jesus, but Jesus knew he needed to go preach the gospel to the other villages: "And they [the disciples] found him and said to him, 'Everyone is looking for you.' And he said to them, 'Let us go on to the next towns, that I may preach there also, for that is why I came out'" (Mark 1:37–38). I'm sure the disciples felt awkward telling the adoring crowds that Jesus needed to go elsewhere. If Jesus knew he needed limitations on his time and presence to advance God's agenda, we need to do the same.

Going back to Bobby, we see an unwillingness for him to accept these limitations. He tries to be available to everyone at any time. Until he joyfully accepts his natural boundaries, he cannot multiply. Leadership multiplication is a replication of oneself. Multiplying leaders limit themselves and empower others for leadership responsibilities. Since Bobby does not recognize his limitations, he will never justify spending some time guiding his assistant in crafting a sermon, leading a meeting, organizing a small-group study, or counseling families.

Sadly, because Bobby feels he must have his hand in everything, his ministry goes a mile wide but an inch deep. Stephen Neill's well-known statement, "If everything is mission, nothing is mission" (Neill, 1959, 81) adequately sums up this leadership style. When you try to be a bridge for everyone, you're not going to effectively help anyone. Even though Bobby is single, many married Christian leaders try to keep that same kind of lifestyle while also raising children. Because many leaders overextend for the tyranny of the urgent, they neglect their most important ministry: making disciples at home.

Self-Pressured Peter

Peter Scazzero, in his book *Emotionally Healthy Spirituality*, describes how his unwillingness to accept limitations nearly crushed his family (Scazzero, 2017, 9–12). His wife Geri eventually declared that she was quitting the church and did not think Peter was a good leader. God graciously healed their marriage but not before they addressed many idols of the heart and unhealthy practices.

Peter tells one story that illustrates the danger of overextension. One Sunday, a struggling couple from out-of-town visited their church. Peter felt self-imposed pressure to invite them over for lunch after a full Sunday of worship and ministry. His hopes for a quick counseling session turned into hours and hours of one-sided conversation from their male guest. The longer this man talked, the more the Scazzeros watched their family time slip away.

At some point, Geri, Peter's wife, realized that their toddler daughter was awfully quiet. Not finding her, a panic-stricken Geri called Pete to help her search. They did not find their girl anywhere in the house and thought to look back by the family pool. Fearing the worst, they discovered their daughter…standing in water up to her neck. She was able to balance on her tippy toes, and by God's grace, she had been able to keep her head above water. One slip of a toe, and she would not have survived. Peter warns the reader that his inability to embrace his limitations almost cost his family everything.

If anyone can justify overextending themselves, Christian leaders easily do. We're so busy helping others with their emergencies, we don't make time for ourselves and our families. Our families, however, bear the weight of our neglect. Barna Research demonstrates a clear statistical connection between leaders at risk for burnout and dissatisfying family relationships (Barna Research, 2017). Too many leaders are too busy to invest in their own families. We overextend ourselves to serve the many but neglect the lives closest to us. However, how we lead in the home impacts how we minister elsewhere (1 Tim 3:5). Our neglect hurts both our testimony and the next generation.

Remember these sobering words from our Christ in Matthew 9: "The harvest is plentiful, but the laborers are few; therefore, pray earnestly to the Lord of the harvest to send out laborers into his harvest" (Matt 9:37–38). Jesus knew we would face a disciple-making and spiritual leadership gap from the beginning. He is not surprised. In his earthly ministry, he faced the pressing demands of leadership more than anyone. He preached, healed, and served so many people. Knowing the needs, he chose to invest much of his time in twelve disciples. He prioritized the growth, discipleship, and leadership development of these men. Through his intentional discipleship, Spirit-empowerment, and leadership multiplication, eleven of these men went on to change the world for Christ.

Based on Jesus' teachings and model, if I want to be a multiplying Christian leader, I must accept three realities. First, this planet has billions of lost and hurting souls in need of Jesus. Second, I must pray for more laborers and fulfill my role in the Great Commission. Third, I must bow the knee to the lordship and direction of Jesus Christ (Matt 28:18). In other words, I need to accept my God-given limitations. By acknowledging my limitations, the need for more laborers, and the lordship of Christ, I can humbly pass the baton of ministry to others.

At the root of Bobby and Peter's issues, we see a great deal of pride. Bobby took pride in being the beloved pastor for his flock. Peter worried about what people would think of him. Proud leaders, however, make terrible multipliers. If I believe the lie that I can single handedly keep the world spinning, I will not multiply. I will handicap or hinder others in kingdom work. Make no mistake, urgent needs will continue to press on us, but God did not call us to bear that pressure alone. Isolation, especially in leadership, was never God's design. Multiplication begins when we realize our own limits and wisely invest our lives into the next generation of leaders.

Living in Isolation

The devil loves isolating the sheep, and too many Christian leaders play right into his hands. At some point, Bobby allowed the ministry to become a substitute for intimate communion with God. Without Christ in the center of his Christian leadership, he lost the heart of ministry altogether. He appeared to care about everyone, but he did not serve ultimately to love Jesus or others. How many fires we extinguish does not impress God. He cares primarily about how much we love him (Mark 12:30–31).

Paul Tripp warns of the dangers of ministry substitution in his book *Dangerous Calling*. He counseled many battered leaders who became consumed with ministry to return to intimacy with Christ. They made their ministry "about budgets, strategic plans, and ministry partnerships. None of these things are wrong in themselves. Many of them are essential. But they must never be the ends in themselves…his heart needs to be tenderized day after day by his communion with Christ so that he becomes a tender, loving, patient, forgiving, encouraging, and giving servant leader" (Tripp, 2012, 63). Jesus loves you, leader, and he created you to know and enjoy him. Out of the overflow of our love for Jesus, we love and serve others.

Bobby did not spend quality time with Jesus, and he did not spend quality time with other believers either. If he wasn't solving a problem, he struggled to justify sitting and simply being with people. He forgot the necessity of human relationships for his health and growth. Jesus will never demand that his disciples abandon gospel community to lead in ministry. Healthy leadership cultivates healthy community, which advances the mission. The idea that one should minister alone did not originate with God.

I fear the main reason many Christian leaders do not invest into others: we offer them only a piece of our selves. We do not fully open up and share. We cannot multiply if we do not sow into the lives of others. God calls us to lead through strong personal relationships. Consider the last time you had a quality conversation with someone that did not center on growing your ministry or business. Are you an active listener, or do you rush conversations to get to your next task? God wants to teach us so many things that can only take place in healthy relationships with other believers. To continually grow and develop as Christians and leaders, we need other people! We must slow down long enough to enjoy God's people. If we prioritize relationships as Jesus did, we will see more fruit in the long term. Healthy multiplication is a fruit of authentic community.

Failing To Plan

We've all heard the adage, "Failing to plan is planning to fail." Quite simply, you cannot call something a priority if you do not make time in your schedule for it. Bobby failed to make time to develop leaders, but he is not alone. As a church planter, I face this tension on an ongoing basis. Planters are constantly making decisions, exploring new ministry opportunities, touring meeting spaces, plugging in volunteers, and planning worship and outreach. I'm sure I sound arrogant saying this, but I feel like if any Christian leader should get a pass at neglecting to develop leaders, it's a church planter. We don't have time to plan for the future because we're trying to solve a million challenges today.

However, if we look at the numbers, we will see that church planters must spend more time developing leaders, not less. Church plants do not always take and about one in three will not make it to year five. However, the odds of survivability in a church plant increase by over 250% where leadership development training is offered (Stetzer and Bird, 2008). If church planters overextend themselves without developing new leaders, they compound the problems. To see a greater harvest, we need stronger roots. In fact, a growing ministry that lacks healthy leadership is not a healthy ministry. I firmly believe in church multiplication, but we cannot multiply healthy churches without healthy leaders.

In the proverbial kitchen of many ministries, we are keeping leadership development on the backburner. At some point, we've got to move leadership development to the front of the stove. We must recognize leadership development as an essential ingredient in God's recipe to make disciples for his kingdom. Jesus developed his disciples in gospel ministry to advance God's kingdom. From day one, he fully invested his life into twelve men. They got all of him, and he wanted all of them. He refused to surrender his Mandate or Commission in the face of mounting public demands.

Let's stop being willing captives to a hurrying Christian ministry. Jesus is our only Master. If we truly believe our leadership exists to serve him, we will make time to invest in others and help them join God in his kingdom agenda. We must choose to bridge the gap and develop leaders in our ministries. We cannot wait for others to take the first step across the gap. God is calling today's Christian leaders to be a bridge to the next generation.

Now that we have more clarity on God's design for healthy leadership and our own propensity to neglect this call, let's look at how Jesus developed leaders. We may find that our current ministry style overlooks this essential aspect of the Great Commission.

3

NEGLECTING THE GREAT COMMISSION

INTENTIONAL DISCIPLESHIP LEADS TO MULTIPLICATION

"And Jesus came and said to them, 'All authority in heaven and on earth has been given to me. Go therefore and make disciples of all nations, baptizing them in the name of the Father and of the Son and of the Holy Spirit, teaching them to observe all that I have commanded you. And behold, I am with you always, to the end of the age'" (Matt 28:18–20).

A growing deficit of healthy Christian leaders reveals cracks in multiple stages of traditional disciple-making methods. Many church-going Christians neglect opening their mouths and sharing the gospel. If they do evangelize, they may limit such conversations to special events or outreaches sponsored by the church. Some churches treat the Sunday sermon as the primary time of discipling. Other churches limit leadership training to annual conferences or weekenders. Over the course of his ministry, however, Jesus demonstrated a holistic and intentional pathway for a disciple's spiritual and leadership development. Jesus proved highly efficient at multiplying healthy Christian leaders because he was also highly intentional in his disciple-making. Today's leaders cannot microwave disciples and expect to develop healthy, multiplying leaders.

Microwaving the Faith of the Next Generation

I'll never forget one time I witnessed this problem. I was volunteering as an FCA (Fellowship of Christian Athletes) chaplain to a football team in a rural Southern county. A former football player myself, I thoroughly enjoyed connecting with these young men and watching their games. I also sought to build relationships with them during their weightlifting sessions, pre-season practices, and pre-game chapels.

Similar to the football program's pattern of preparation for the season, I sought to help these players grow in the Word continually. Whether in large-group or one-on-one settings, these evangelism and discipleship opportunities slowly began to yield fruit. It took time to build trust, and I didn't always get it right, but God showed me that these incredible young men had potential for Christ.

One week, the schedule worked out where another local pastor and a traveling evangelist could come and share the Word for chapel. The team and coaches gathered in the upper meeting room like we typically did. After the introductions, the evangelist shared his testimony and gave a passionate evangelistic message. I appreciated the eagerness to share the good news. However, at the conclusion of his message, the evangelist called the players to suddenly raise their hands if they wanted to "accept Jesus." It was a confusing call to action, but dozens of players quickly raised their hands. The evangelist thanked God for those hands, wrapped up his message, and the chapel service ended. I did not hear him offer to help anyone take further steps in their spiritual journey. The next day, he and the pastor gleefully reported to the church that dozens of football players put their faith in Jesus. The church erupted in applause.

At first, I also wanted to share the excitement. Even if the altar call was confusing, I hoped some of those young men understood and trusted Christ. The next time we held chapel, however, I found a different outcome entirely. I told the group, "I saw that some of you raised your hand to say you put your faith in Jesus last week. I'd like to follow up with you after chapel and help you take the next step in your faith journey." I waited after the chapel expecting a handful of players to follow up. Not one player came to talk with me. Worse, I saw no new players publicly profess Christ, get baptized, or take a visible step in their Christian faith as a result of raising their hands. I'll never forget that moment of realization when I witnessed an attempt to microwave disciples. While I was heartbroken over my experience with FCA, this scene is by no means an isolated incident in the Christian world today.

Making disciples, like having children, goes beyond the moment of conception and requires time and teaching for believers to reach their fullest potential. Microwaving disciples does not lead to healthy, multiplying leaders. We have to look beyond the ingredients of disciple-making (going, baptizing, teaching); we also need to observe how Jesus discipled his disciples. Jesus shows us how to become an intentional disciple-maker who leads others into deep transformation and leadership development.

Intentional Discipleship

Before Jesus gave the Great Commission, he first gave the example of his life, teachings, and ministry. In other words, when he told his disciples to "make disciples" he quantified that term. Mark 3:13–19 shows the way Jesus selected, instructed, and equipped his disciples for ministry. Jesus set apart twelve to follow him more closely in what you might call a small group. From the beginning, Jesus had the end goal of multiplying his disciples for his kingdom. His missional small group became the avenue for that process.

I love turning to the Gospel According to Mark for several reasons. For one, Mark shows Jesus as the Son of Man with authority but who used his authority to serve and to save. Also, Mark emphasizes personal discipleship in his gospel account. In fact, after announcing that it was time to "repent and believe in the gospel" (1:15b), the next words Mark records Jesus as saying are, "Follow me, and I will make you fishers of men" (1:17). True to his word, Jesus did not merely attract followers. He reproduced fishers of men.

As we look to the Master, we see the best paradigm for disciple-making. Jesus did not focus on rapid growth or addition to his flock. In fact, he often drove the flighty crowds away with his explicit gospel messages (John 6:66). He called his disciples because he was fully invested in their lives. Jesus shows us through intentional discipleship that we must replicate through pursuing personal proximity, prioritizing people, and propelling pacesetters.

Personal Proximity

Before selecting his disciples, Jesus spent much time in prayer with his Father (Luke 6:12). His intimacy with the Father led him to invite twelve specific men to follow him and "be with him" (3:14). Jesus's decision to personally call his disciples contrasts with the rabbinical tradition of the day in which disciples sought out their teacher. The busy Lord slowed down to invite these men into his life and ministry. He could not invest in every follower the same way, but he intentionally planned to invest deeply in these men. He gave the greatest gift possible to his group: himself!

Jesus desired the disciples to "be with him" because he loved them. In *Lead Like Jesus*, Ken Blanchard says that "love draws us into relationships" (Blanchard, Hodges, and Hendry, 2016, 91). Jesus knew the disciples intimately and wanted them to grow in the knowledge of him. He redeemed and transformed their lives as they did. Christ taught his twelve, fed them, answered their questions, and explained the ways of the kingdom of God. They asked him how to pray, and he showed them how to speak with the Father. He continued to love them even to the end when they were faithless or left him alone to die (John 13:1, 21). We cannot think of biblical discipleship without a context of authentic community and personal relationships (Kell, 2012).

Christian leaders must view discipling others by the word of God as our primary calling (Matt 28:20). So, no matter where we lead, we must love Jesus so deeply that we treasure his every word and love others so much that we commit our lives to sharing his truth with them. We cannot divorce true Christian development from proximity to Jesus and others.

When we make time to invest God's Word and spiritual gifts into others, in his timing, God brings the multiplication. Jesus does not want us to be Christian-adding factories devoid of authentic love. He desires quality disciples who require quality time investment from other disciples. We must replicate the Word-centered ministry of Jesus and his unending patience to chisel the most obsolete and wayward people into trophies of grace. Spiritual maturity comes slowly and requires much correction, instruction, and grace along the way (Ps 27:17). Such a life-on-life discipleship process requires proximity and time.

A church leader who desires to model the ministry of Jesus will need to pursue a ministry of proximity. Jesus ate with sinners, invited people into his presence, and showed grace when their desperation resulted in disruption (Mark 2:1–5). He gave the apostles unfettered access to his life and ministry (Mark 1:21–28, 1:40–45, 2:1–12, 2:23–3:6, 4:35–41, 5:35–43, 7:14–23, 8:1–10, 14–21, 10:17–31). Because he entwined his life with his disciples, he had the opportunity to preach to them in every season of life and ministry (John 6:67–68; see also 2 Tim 4:2).

Through the ministry of presence, Jesus answered questions, rebuked, assessed, coached, and praised the twelve. He exemplified a leader who intentionally developed leaders for the multiplication of disciples in the church. He invested his time in others, and his church should reflect such investment.

More and more Christian leaders are trending away from local church ministry to produce online content as their primary ministry. Moving away from messy people might be easier for creating content, but it's unsustainable for healthy multiplication. Multiplying leaders will take time, week after week, nurturing and discipling willing mentees under their care. God made us to work through us! In the long run, we will see fruitful multiplication (Matt 13:8). Discipleship may take time away from other pressing projects, but because Jesus modeled the value of personal presence, we must as well.

Prioritizing People

Jesus came not only to preach the good news of the kingdom but also to make time to equip his followers for a lifetime of ministry. I love that Jesus called these twelve ordinary men (most of them teenagers) to immediately preach and to cast out demons. He knew them and cared enough to entrust his very life and ministry in their young hands. They were young and inexperienced. They doubted Jesus on many occasions. Still, Jesus intentionally used their personalities and giftings to serve others. In his kingdom, he views people as prized and useful.

Christ selflessly used the context of his ministry to develop his followers to use their gifts and abilities for the kingdom of God. He did not call the already qualified because he planned to equip the called. He taught them the Word and sent them out to the villages to preach and prepare the people. He ministered not alongside the academics or religious elite but the fishermen, tax collectors, and political zealots.

Not limiting himself to preachers, Jesus did the same for those with the most meager gifts and social standing. In one case, an unnamed woman anointed Jesus's feet with every ounce of her extravagant perfume (Mark 14:3–9). The disciples saw no value in her offering. Judas Iscariot recognized a loss of financial gain and personal interest. Jesus saw something infinitely more valuable in her heart of faith. He saw how she trusted his Word about the cross and anticipated his sacrificial death. She sacrificed what she could in preparation of his offering. He taught the roomful of men, "Truly, I say to you, wherever the gospel is proclaimed in the whole world, what she has done will be told in memory of her" (14:9). Even as an unnamed witness for Christ, the example of this woman would echo for eternity.

To develop people like Jesus, the church must first and foremost prioritize people. Jesus Christ demonstrated the power of the kingdom of God when he got ahold of a disciple's life. Godly leaders must have a love for others that endures, hopes, and invests even if it does not benefit us. We shouldn't ask people to join us to see what we can get out of them. We want to see what God wants to make of them. Jesus did not hoard people for his personal projects; he sought to transform and empower them.

Leaders must intentionally call people to develop them as far along as we can. Spiritual leaders do not wait for believers to mature before they initiate development. As they love and pursue others, they will see kingdom potential become reality. As Aubrey Malphurs and Will Mancini encourage, a developer of leaders must be willing to "take up the towel rather than throw in the towel" (Malphurs and Mancini, 2004, 21). Likewise, leader developers must be willing to prioritize people and see their potential.

This eternal perspective requires sacrifice but yields eternal rewards. You might not see the blessings when people demand your time or flake on their opportunities. If you're introverted or task-oriented, you might feel the pinch even more. However, I can testify to the power of leaders willing to invest in me.

In high school, I had two youth pastors (Dwayne and Dan) who chose to personally invest in me. As they discipled teenage me, they also invited me to start using my gifts in music and leadership. It's embarrassing to admit, but I did not do a great job leading music. In fact, one time I concluded a worship song on a minor chord. Not knowing what to do, I went ahead and sat down. Since the song didn't resolve in anyone's head, the youth pastor led everyone in a closing chorus a cappella. On another occasion, I started to lead a game of "Simon Says" only to shortly realize that I cannot do two things at once. I froze, couldn't think of any more motions, and abdicated the game leading to another youth leader. Another time, I was asked to speak on the fifth day of creation to a group of elementary children. To no fault of my youth pastor, I did not prepare well or know how to communicate effectively with the kids. I finished my content in two minutes and rambled for the rest of the time.

I would totally understand if these youth leaders decided to stop giving me chances to lead. I didn't deserve them. Dwayne and Dan had compassion and wanted God to use me. They made opportunities to allow me to lead something that they would have undoubtedly done better. They prioritized people because they prioritized me. By God's grace, and continual investment, I've grown in Christ and my service capability. I could tell you stories from many other seasons in my life where Christian leaders prioritized me. I'm able to preach the Word, counsel, lead singing, disciple others, and serve my family as a husband and father. I could not do any of these things without patient models.

Like Jesus, these leaders discipled and equipped me in as many aspects of my Christian walk as they could. Next, they propelled me to go out into the world and make disciples and leaders of the next generation. Jesus set the example by passing the baton onto the eleven faithful disciples. If the perfect Son of God is willing to propel his disciples to set a new pace and reach new frontiers for the kingdom of God, so should we.

Propel Pacesetters

Jesus transformed the lives of eleven of those disciples and patiently developed them into apostles who led the early church to multiply throughout the known world. The significant office of apostle established the New Testament church. These men testified of the resurrection of Jesus Christ and the powerful coming of his Spirit. Jesus poured into these men for approximately three years, but when the climactic moment came to usher in the church era, Jesus was not there. He told the disciples, "It is to your advantage that I go away" (John 16:7). Jesus needed to ascend the throne of heaven, so he chose for his disciples to carry on his work in the flesh for this new chapter in redemptive history.

From the beginning, he sent out the disciples to "preach and have authority to cast out demons" (Mark 3:14b–15). Mark Strauss explains, "This is the same ministry that Jesus has been performing" (Strauss, 2017). The apostles functioned as messengers who went out and replicated the powerful ministry of Jesus. The infinitive of κηρύσσω translates as "to preach," which means that the apostles had a similar proclamation ministry as John the Baptist, Jesus, and those miraculously healed (Guelich, 1989, 159).

Through his resurrection, Jesus empowered others to step up in new ways and use their voices to advance his gospel message. A group of women served as the first witnesses of his resurrection power. Because the disciples hid and disbelieved Christ's promises, they missed out on a great blessing. The women testified boldly as witnesses to Jesus's resurrection hope. Legally speaking, women were not allowed to serve as witnesses in the Jewish legal system. But in Jesus's kingdom, he called them to cross this man-made boundary and lead others to the empty tomb.

Does God call every Christian to spiritual leadership? If you think of spiritual leaders as only apostles, pastors, and deacons, then no. If you see spiritual leadership as an extension of the Great Commission, where believers use their gifts to glorify God to the max and address the needs of others, then the answer must be absolutely YES. Jesus did not call his disciples to hold his luggage while he did the important work. To him, developing these men to help spread the gospel *was* the important work and the inevitable result of intentional discipleship.

Can you believe that Jesus calls us to represent him and carry on his ministry? What an honor! If we cannot joyfully set others free to follow God's calling on their lives, we're not multiplying leaders. Certainly, they will not lead exactly like we do, but we must trust God's design. If he can use messed up people like us, then the hope for the next generation is even greater! Remember that the disciples failed Jesus in his darkest hour, but he forgave them and recommissioned them for service. God's grace trumps any failure. By his grace, he propelled them to step out by faith and spread the gospel to the ends of the earth. With the power of the Holy Spirit, they started new churches, ministries, and multiplied disciples. The book of Acts is evidence that the gospel work continued through Jesus's servant leaders to the next generation and beyond.

Many Christian organizations I know do a good job of helping people, and I thank God for that. But are we doing a good job of developing people like Jesus did? Are we teaching them how to do the important work of serving God to the max? Or do we simply hand out fishing poles and tell people to keep fishing under our supervision indefinitely? Jesus demonstrated complete selflessness and multiplied Christian leaders to new horizons.

It's time to see potential in people the way that God does. We exist to propel people to do God's kingdom work. God never calls us to disciple people beyond our capability or force others to take on roles they are not ready for, but he does call us to fully invest and send out. To reach new horizons for the next generation, we need to invest our lives building bridges of new Christian leaders. If you want to be a part of God's plans into the future, you'll invest in people the way Jesus did. So how do we reassess our leadership and adjust towards God's plans? That's where we turn next.

Application Questions

- Where do you find yourself neglecting aspects of the Great Commission? Do you have close proximity to other believers who can encourage and help you grow?
- What abilities has God given you to influence people for Christ? What are your social circles or different spheres of influence?

- In what ways can you build leadership development into those spheres of influence?
- If you replicated a disciple with your current passion and obedience for Christ, what would they look like? What gets the majority of your time and passion these days? How can you better align your weekly priorities with the mission of God?
- What weekly responsibilities can you turn into disciple-making opportunities?

4

REASSESSMENT AND ADAPTATION
SHIFTING FROM BURNOUT TO MULTIPLICATION

"We've never done it that way before." These words can be the final epitaph for a dying organization or a great opportunity to discover a new path forward. As we rediscover God's plan for multiplying healthy leaders, we're sure to notice our own shortcomings. No one hits the mark perfectly. But Jesus—He knows our shortcomings and continually gives us grace to repent and get closer to him and get on his agenda.

Today's Christian leaders have important questions before them. What should we do about our neglect to multiply healthy leaders? What do we need to do to ensure the future of the American church?

We must reassess and adapt!

Moses, one of the greatest prophets in redemptive history, provides an enduring example for today's Christian leaders. Even though Moses made some enormous mistakes in his life, God gave him a gracious awareness of those mistakes, and Moses humbly repented and changed his ways. At a pivotal moment for Israel's leadership and judicial system in Exodus 18, God turned a crisis into a multiplying movement of healthy leaders. Growth requires change, and Moses serves as an excellent example for Christian leaders when we need to adapt our ministry to multiply healthy leaders.

Leading a New Nation

At the outset of Exodus, the Hebrew people were in trouble. The Egyptians enslaved the Hebrews and forced them into servitude and suffering for many years. They cried out for deliverance, and God heard their cries. God chose to use an unlikely man named Moses as his mouthpiece to Pharaoh and the Israelites and to perform mighty works demonstrating God's existence and superior power to the Egyptian gods. Moses, a Hebrew raised in the house of Pharaoh, murdered an Egyptian and then ran away to the land of Midian. He became a shepherd and settled down for forty years in relative obscurity. God chose to reveal himself to Moses and called him to bring millions of Israelites out of captivity to worship the living God. Imagine what Moses felt at the age of 80 when his calling transferred from shepherding a literal herd of sheep to shepherding a flock of over a million people!

After the miraculous crossing of the Red Sea, the people journeyed into the wilderness without a government, book of law, or judicial system. They primarily looked to one human shepherd named Moses for guidance. They depended fully on his dispensation of Yahweh's wisdom for their spiritual and judicial needs. Moses faced a unique leadership challenge, which almost became a crisis in Exodus 18:13–27. He led God's people to the best of his ability, but his neglect to raise up additional leaders hampered the development of his people and his own health.

A Recipe for Burnout

When Moses's father-in-law, Jethro, joined up with the traveling nation in Exodus 18, he stayed to observe his son-in-law at work in his new leadership role. He watched Moses work incredibly hard to shepherd Israel all through the daylight hours, but Jethro noticed a looming organizational crisis in Moses's current strategy (Meyers, 2005, 135). Moses responded to the growing needs by attempting to do too much for the people and overextending himself. Jethro, an experienced Midianite leader (Exod 3:1), knew something needed to change and scheduled a "come to Jesus meeting" with his son-in-law.

Jethro asked Moses, "What is this that you are doing for the people? Why do you sit alone, and all the people stand around you from morning till evening?" (Exod 18:13–14). Jethro did not chide Moses for listening to the problems in the camp and judging over the people. Historically, a political or military leader like Moses customarily would also function as a judicial leader. Jethro said that the first problem of Moses's judgment was that he tried to sit and judge *alone*. His solitary leadership created a backlog in the volume of cases, so when evening came, scores of people went home without a proper hearing or receiving justice in a reasonable time span. Moses could not keep up with the crying demands for justice. Because Jethro cared about Moses, he pointed out this blind spot.

Another symptom of overextension Jethro noticed was Moses's continual emotional and physical exhaustion. The Hebrew word נבל [*nabel*], which translates to "wear oneself out," gives the idea that Moses was sinking down from that exhaustion (Hamilton, 2011, 283). Today, we could call this burnout. Moses's weariness was self-inflicted, and by making the people stand around all day begging for his attention, they wore out as well. Jethro frankly said,

"What you are doing is not good. You and the people with you will certainly wear yourselves out, for the thing is too heavy for you. You are not able to do it alone" (Exod 18:17–18). Moses was trying to do it all by himself and his health, influence, and flock suffered for it. Thankfully, Moses received Jethro's counsel, and God turned this period of burnout into a blessing.

Moses Accepted Help

Like Moses, many Christian leaders today try to manage most issues themselves. Scripture, however, shows a foundational truth: God did not create one man to manage everything (Gen 2:18). Because of pride, humans push past the limits healthy, God-given boundaries. We're tempted to ignore outside counsel, downplay problems, or look through rose-colored glasses. It was painful for Moses to receive a critical evaluation of his ministry. Even more humbling, God used Jethro, Moses's father-in-law, to deliver that message. Despite any discomfort Moses felt, God faithfully gave Moses every measure of grace and help for his life and ministry calling.

Exodus centers on the rescuing power and covenant faithfulness of Yahweh God. God revealed his personal covenant name to Moses as Yahweh, or "I AM that I AM" (Exod. 3:14). Clearly, the only self-sufficient character in this entire redemptive narrative is God (Exod. 3:14; 18:18). Israel hit a wall in their slavery conditions, and when they had nowhere else to turn, they cried out to God for help. Yahweh God could have led his own people out of Egypt. He did not need Moses, but Moses and Israel certainly needed him. Moses, however, still hit a wall in his leadership in Exodus 18 and needed to make a change. Sometimes, God allows leaders to hit a wall for us to acknowledge our limitations and reach outside ourselves to him and the resources he gives us.

Moses's response to this leadership challenge demonstrated a lot about his character and leadership focus. Because he was willing to reassess the focus of his ministry, he shifted from leadership fatigue and burnout to healthy multiplication. If we want to experience the fullest blessings of God's plan for our ministries, we would do well to reassess how we get things done. Moses adapted to become a healthy, multiplying leader because he exhibited three vital heart qualities.

Qualities of an Adapting Leader

#1: Humility

The first quality of Moses's adaptive leadership was humility. He did not argue or defend his leadership choices to Jethro. He made room at the table for an outside consultant to critique his way of doing things. He listened well and accepted the responsibility for the changes. Though the text does not use the term "repent," clearly, Moses changed his ways. Humble repentance, especially in positions of leadership, enables leaders to grow and mature spiritually while setting a godly example for others.

Moses not only took Jethro's recommendations to heart but also implemented those changes shortly afterwards. While the feeling of burnout may have motivated his quick response, Moses knew that he did not have all the answers, which allowed him to receive wisdom at the right time to help his people. Proud leaders refuse to change. We must resist the desire to justify our lackluster people-development record and keep doing things the same way. We know something needs to change, but we must humbly realize that we ourselves must change first.

God gave Moses the eagerness to adapt and bring others into his ministry. He didn't view these new judges as charity cases. These new judges were qualified leaders, with the more respected and capable men being entrusted with even greater responsibilities. The humility of Moses allowed him to affirm and encourage the giftedness of others without feeling threatened or diminished in his role. Such humility is necessary for healthy, long-term spiritual leadership and the health of our organizations. Doing things the same way methodologically will lead to inevitable decline.

Blockbuster Video serves as a cautionary tale for leaders who do not feel the need to adapt. In the early 2000s, Blockbuster dominated the video rental market with in home DVD and VHS rentals. Worth billions of dollars, the organization thought little of upcoming rivals like Netflix and spent more time worrying about cable companies. When presented with an offer to buy Netflix in 2000 for $50 million, CEO Jim Keyes proudly said, "Neither Redbox nor Netflix are even on the radar screen in terms of competition" (C12, 2022). By 2010, Blockbuster had filed for bankruptcy. As of December 2023, Netflix has a market cap of $198.6 Billion.

Blockbuster would have benefited from a humble evaluation of their competition's methods and value. Moses faced no competition in his role but had the same choice: humbly accept help or figure things out on his own. Too many of us keep doing the latter, and we must repent of that mentality today. As Zack Eswine wrote, "You and I were never meant to repent for not being everywhere for everybody and all at once. You and I are meant to repent because we've tried to be" (Eswine, 2015, 74).

#2: Teachability

Moses's adapting leadership also provides an example of teachability. Every leader needs to continually learn and grow to better serve others. At this point in his life, Moses was over eighty years old. Few people enjoy making significant changes in the way they do things at that age. Moses, however, listened intently as Jethro taught him how to appoint new leader judges and what their qualifications should be (Exod 18:21). Jethro advised looking for capable, God-fearing, trustworthy, and honest men. He told Moses to set them over groups of thousands, hundreds, fifties, and tens (18:25). This new system took a great reorganization effort but allowed quicker access to justice for the people and a built-in appeals process.

Moses eagerly adapted to the new operating system and set about the training process. He slowed down to learn to do something better, and as a result, he multiplied new spiritual leaders. He did not allow himself to feel threatened or argue how the old ways worked just fine. Instead, he moved to action. If Moses refused Jethro's counsel, he would have hindered the people and his own opportunity to lead. Leaders with no feedback or honest accountability can easily drive themselves and/or their people into the ground or off mission. God spoke through Jethro's timely advice, and Moses recognized his voice with a teachable spirit. His example shows how teachable leaders will always benefit the people they influence.

#3: Word-Centered

Moses displayed a third adaptive quality. He was burdened to keep the word of God front and center. Moses said his underlying desire for rendering all judgments was to see justice accomplished with the people (Exod 18:15). When people brought problems, he saw discipleship opportunities. Though he overextended himself, he took the responsibility to personally instruct the people in God's word (18:16). Once he noticed his approach was slowing the spread of the word, Moses pivoted and appointed new leaders so that the people received more timely help (18:20). Like Jesus's appointment of the apostles and the apostles' appointment of servant leaders in Acts 6, Moses was adamant that the ministry of the word must continue.

Because the ministry of the word comes first, Christian leaders can and should adapt their methods, as needs change based on the context and people we're trying to help. Since we're trying to help the next generation, let's look at Generation Z, (those born from 1996–2012). Surveys show this generation wants to make a difference in this world. They value purpose and commitment, even over the amount of money they make (Perna, 2019). They also care to help the underserved and marginalized people groups. Christian leaders should embrace the differences of this generation and adapt to help them discover and live out God's plan for their lives. Using the example of Moses, today's Christian leaders need to see the heart of this next generation and help them to center their values and purpose on the Word of God. God's enduring Word speaks to any generation at any time! With the lens of God's agenda, we can see the potential for God's kingdom to advance in incredible ways.

Looking for Sleeping Leaders

When I served as a student pastor, I thought I had my methods down. I preached the Word every Wednesday night, equipped adult leaders to teach the Word on Sunday morning, and planned retreats and outings to help students and families spiritually. We had many students in the ministry. I had a full plate and thought I was doing a pretty good job developing leaders. To humble me, God gave me a sleeping leader: Literally and figuratively!

Every time I preached the Word to the youth group on Wednesdays, I would see one of our adult leaders, a young man in his 20s named Danny (not his real name), fall asleep. I knew my preaching might not be that exciting, but I began to get a little offended. He wasn't even trying to hide his drowsiness! Could he not see how important the teaching of God's word was to student ministry?

I wasn't sure what to do, and I didn't want to embarrass him, so I asked Danny to get lunch with me one day. As we talked, God opened my eyes to understand him. Personality wise, Danny never fit the mold of a classroom learner. He worked the night shift as an assistant manager at a local grocery store. Even though he was exhausted every Wednesday evening, he came to church faithfully and served each week. I became deeply thankful for his commitment and wondered if I would have the level of commitment he demonstrated if I were in his shoes.

I realized that the teaching of the Word is central, but perhaps I could adapt certain elements of our ministry to better equip Danny to serve. First, I felt led to meet one-on-one with him for accountability and discipleship. As we grew closer in friendship and as ministry partners, Danny willingly volunteered to help me with any hands-on projects. I discovered his greatest strengths involved physical activity. I never doubted that anytime I needed help moving a heavy load or setting up for a church activity, I could call on Danny.

Second, as I trusted his knowledge of the Word and Christian example, I encouraged him to lead a middle school guys discussion group. Working alongside Danny opened my mind to the thought that we could do a better job reaching the next generation by creating focused small groups on Sunday nights. Unlike Sunday school and Wednesday nights, which primarily featured auditory learning, these groups made disciples through engagement and hands-on learning. I encouraged our adult leaders to use their gifts and passions to discover a focus for their groups. One leader started a prayer group. Another leader started a worship leadership group. Still another started a group for those who felt called to the ministry. Another leader led a group to serve at a local senior adult home. The students eagerly responded to these new ministry groups by signing up and inviting their friends. We saw our students grow closer together, leaders develop leaders, and the next generation empowered for ministry.

I witnessed the blessing of seeing God do something great in the next generation. It all started with my humbling experience with a sleeping leader.

God softened my heart so that I could see something needed to change. I had to adapt my methods to better equip people for ministry. When I let go of my plans and my feelings and centered the program on God's agenda for developing people, he did so much more than I could have asked or imagined.

Leaders, we're entrusted with God's Word for such a time as this. We serve at his pleasure and for the good of those around us. Let's not be controlling leaders who refuse to change or delegate ministry responsibilities to others out of exhaustion. Multiplying leaders equip others to share the Word of God for the maximum benefit of all people. When we open our hearts to doing things God's way, we will witness the gospel advance, believers strengthened, the next generation empowered, and leaders multiplied.

Look in the Mirror

Once Moses shifted his thinking, Israel experienced a multiplication of thousands of leaders who could use their gifts and abilities to serve the people and glorify God. What if God wants to do the greatest gospel advancing work in our lifetime, but we're too stuck in our ways to see it? Without humility, a teachable spirit, or Word-centered ministry, we may burnout or bottleneck God's plan for those around us. The adaptive qualities serve as a helpful mirror for us to evaluate our hearts. God does not need leadership gurus; he desires humble and available servants. You don't need a PhD to see a leader multiplying movement, but you do need the heart of a learner.

God gave you unique gifts but most importantly, he gave you a calling: to make disciples of all nations and multiply leaders for the next generation. It's time to start changing the way we lead so we can serve as better examples for the next generation of men and women. To reach them, we must first bow the knee to God's plan and repent of our selfishness and pride. We must acknowledge that we can too easily reject instruction from others or get stuck in our ways.

At the same time, we must realize that Jesus loves us so much and is quick to forgive. Where sin abounds, grace abounds all the more (Rom 5:20). When we take his instructions to heart and change our ways, we will see him accomplish more than we ever imagined. We will experience the joy of being a part of his plan. A heart of humility is the starting place.

I want to help guide you to the point where you become a healthy, multiplying leader for Christ. I've provided an assessment tool that I want you to pray over and use as a mirror for your heart. How are you *really* doing at multiplying Christian leaders? Where we fall short, let's repent and seek help together.

Dear God, forgive us for being too busy to see the potential in sleeping leaders all around us. Help us to see ourselves honestly. Help us to lead others differently.

Healthy, Multiplying Leadership Assessment

Take this Self-Assessment for an Honest Evaluation of Your Leadership.

For honest feedback, ask a "Jethro" to look over your answers. If married, ask your spouse for a review of your responses. Thoughtfully answer the statements below with one of the following responses: Never–Sporadic–Frequent

Spiritual Health

- You spend quality time with the Father in the Word and prayer throughout the week.
- You routinely take time to hear from God through corporate worship and prayer.
- At least once a month you talk to a mature believer to receive mentoring in the faith.
- You do not find yourself frequently serving with a rushed or anxious state of mind.
- You dedicate time each week to fulfill the Great Commission through:

    Evangelizing the Lost
    Discipling Believers
    Equipping Others
    Developing Leaders

- People look to you to consistently model the virtuous leadership of Christ and fruit of the Spirit.
- You genuinely enjoy serving the Lord and others in your current capacity.

- You set at least one day aside for rest from work and get enough sleep each night.
- You read at least one book a month to develop your thinking and grow.

Relational Health

- You gather in groups led by other believers for mutual encouragement and intentional discipleship.
- You look to connect with others outside of mandatory work meetings and functions.
- You show grace to your team when they mess up and handle criticism with emotional maturity.
- You listen well to others and ask regularly "What is God doing in your life?"
- You invite the Holy Spirit to interrupt your daily agenda to help others.
- When a teachable person in your organization asks for an hour of your time, you prioritize that meeting.
- You hold gifted leaders to the standards and core values your organization has set.
- You invite peers or mentors to point out your blind spots in matters of Christian life or leadership.
- You read the Bible and pray with your family and prioritize their faith development.
- Your spouse and children enjoy serving Jesus alongside you.

Replicating Leadership

- If you get hit by a bus, you have leaders trained and prepared to carry out responsibilities in your absence.
- You can trust other capable leaders to take initiative without micromanagement.
- You take others along with you to serve or provide opportunities within your sphere of influence (leading meetings, organizing new initiatives, etc).
- You prepare others well for the tasks you delegate to them.
- You regularly assess the effectiveness of your ministry and accept coaching to help you grow.
- Ten percent of your weekly schedule (or more) is dedicated to raising up the next generation of leaders.
- You host or highlight equipping and training opportunities to help others be successful.
- People in your sphere of influence often achieve new levels of leadership capacity.
- The people in your previous workplaces or ministries describe you as a leader developer.
- Most of your best leaders were developed within your organization.
- You celebrate when God calls others to a new ministry even when they must leave your organization to do so.
- Your ministry or organization has intentionally replicated a new group with new leadership within the last year.

Post-Assessment Reflection

- What areas are you most encouraged to see God working through you?
- What areas of your life and leadership do you see that are struggling or neglecting kingdom priorities?
- What were the biggest disconnects between your self-perception and your spouse or mentor's impressions?

5

THE MARKS OF A MULTIPLYING LEADER

HEALTHY LEADERS DEVELOP HEALTHY LEADERS

If you have ever flown on an airplane, you know the drill: the flight attendants instruct passengers that in the unlikely event of an emergency, oxygen masks will deploy over each seat. However, the next part often defies every parent's instinct. They tell you to put your own oxygen mask on first before assisting others. This procedure has metaphorical applications to many arenas of life, especially healthy Christian leadership. We cannot fully help others grow until we have attended to our own growth.

If you did not take the time to complete your leadership self-assessment, please turn back a few pages and complete it now. Until we honestly assess our own health and leadership track record, we cannot and should not tell others where they need to grow. We need clarity on our own shortcomings to redirect ourselves and ministries to God's agenda. By God's grace, he will change us to be more like Jesus as disciples and leaders.

Ultimately, we cannot multiply what we do not possess. While we could overlook our own heart issues and start creating leadership pathways and training events, God does not condone such efforts.

Shiny new strategies and lofty visions do not cultivate healthy next-generation multiplication. Scott Boren says that too often "leadership training focuses on the 'how' instead of the 'who'" (Boren, 2010). Christian leaders must realize the truth: training programs cannot reproduce Christian leaders; Christian leaders reproduce leaders.

What kind of leaders *consistently* reproduce healthy leaders? If we want to start a movement of healthy multiplication, we need to first ask God to help produce the right qualities in us. Only then will we be able to identify and equip other potential leaders.

In my doctoral research, I found leading experts on Christian small groups and multiplication who agreed on five characteristics common to multiplying leaders.

Replicating leaders consistently show five characteristics:

1. Spiritually Healthy
2. Mature in the Faith
3. Shepherd Leaders
4. Persistent in Prayer
5. Trusting Delegators

Spiritually Healthy

The call to be spiritually healthy leaders might seem redundant at this point in the book, but the stakes are too high to get this wrong. I've seen leaders eagerly delegate responsibilities to leaders with strong personalities or strong aspirations but not with strong spiritual health. These situations often proved disastrous for the leaders and the people. We cannot prioritize expansion at the expense of spiritual intimacy. God calls us to empower the next generation to know and become like Christ. As we cling to him and work out our faith in front of others, we can better pass on the baton to the next generation. Spiritual leadership development and replication, however, flows out of our own spiritual health.

Spiritually healthy leaders love Jesus and his church. Don Whitney defines spiritual health with Christ as the center: "As Jesus is the source of spiritual life, so he also is the standard of spiritual health" (Whitney, 2001). In his book, *Home Cell Group Explosion*, Joel Comiskey shares statistical research that indicates leaders who spend more time with God often lead groups that grow faster (Comiskey, 2002). People love authenticity, especially authentic Christian leadership.

Scott Boren likewise states that "leaders who pray in daily devotions and in intercession for their group members lead better groups" (Boren, 2014). However, Boren warns that the leader must desire to spend time with Jesus to grow, not merely use his time with Jesus as a means to an end. Spiritual health must remain the leader's priority. Leaders who spend quality time with Jesus and become like him set an excellent example for the next generation.

Boren further draws the connection from spiritual health to missional activity by saying, "It's one thing to do some activities now and then that look loving. It's another thing to be formed into the kind of person who loves. In the first instance, we do things to be effective and maybe even to get credit for making a difference. In the second, we love because we have been formed by the God of love and as a result love flows out of us" (Boren, 2014). Genuinely loving leaders make a difference in others over the course of their lifetime.

Small-group expert Neal McBride notes the trickle-down effect of leadership when he says Jesus' small group of disciples formed the "platform for Jesus' ministry to large groups of people" (McBride,

1990). Out of the depth of their gospel commitments, the disciples influenced many for Christ.

In contrast, spiritually unhealthy leaders create instability in the people they lead. Jeffrey Arnold warns that such leaders "hinder growth, exclude people, provide platforms for negative or destructive personalities and keep people from reaching their potential for service and outreach" (Arnold, 2004, 32). The spiritual health of leaders makes all the difference between multiplying problems or healthy leaders.

Because we lead for the glory of God and the good of others, we cannot neglect our spiritual health for the mission. Jesus shows us his mission: the spiritual health of this generation of disciples and the next generation. Healthy ministries are built one healthy leader at a time (Arnold, 2004, 32). Allow God to change and mature your faith so others under your influence will notice and replicate the difference.

Mature in the Faith

Christian leaders should resist the impulse to take shortcuts to rapidly multiply, especially when considering the responsibilities of leading souls. Too many organizations today are lowering the character standards for their leaders. Scott Boren and Jim Egli warn that lowering standards will "actually work against long-term success" (Boren and Egli, 2014, 163). A mature leader can help nurture and develop healthy leaders in the next generation. Baby leaders are not in a position of strength to multiply.

Steve Gladen, Small Groups Pastor at Saddleback Church and multiplication expert, oversees 3,500 small groups meeting all over the world. He says, "The fundamental issue that determines the extent to which God can bless your leadership is your heart"

(Gladen, 2012, 32). Christian character–not mere aspirations– sets apart leadership that leads toward lasting health and eventually, multiplication. If we care for our leaders, we will want to see them put in a position that truly blesses them and the people they serve. We do not always have to choose between quality or quantity, but if we have to prioritize, we must always choose quality first.

Of course, some will argue that nobody is perfect and use that to justify the deployment of immature leaders. If you think you're helping these people out, you're actually setting them up to fail. As key influencers, leaders live in a bubble. They face increased attacks from the Evil One, and the stakes are much higher. Arnold reminds us that Christian leaders "need to be above reproach so that we can foster the kind of respect that our position dictates, which means guarding against small slips as well as big falls" (Arnold, 2004, 32). A publicized fall can greatly harm leaders and their loved ones.

First Timothy 3:1–7 clearly states church leaders need to resist drunkenness, greed, violence, and other disqualifying lifestyles. All Christian leaders, not just pastors, need to reject these sinful ways. Even a seemingly minor character flaw expands under the scope of leadership.

On the flipside, mature Christian behaviors can influence a group to fully embrace and devote themselves to Christ. Regardless of your personality or skillset, you can make a significant impact if you conduct yourself according to Christ's standards. Remember Paul's instruction on true greatness to Timothy in 1 Timothy 6:6: "but godliness with contentment is great gain."

Shepherd Leaders

Because we care about the long-term feasibility and encouragement of the leaders we propel forward, multiplying leaders think past initial training and deployments. In his book *Leading Small Groups*, Chris Surratt notes that shepherding leadership is a key element in healthy multiplying leaders (Surratt, 2019, 11). Good leaders need to know how to care for their people and cultivate healthy disciple-making and Christian leadership pathways (Hartwig, Davis, and Sniff, 2020, 20). Just as shepherds care for and guide their sheep, shepherd-leaders also care for and guide their protegees.

Ed Stetzer and Eric Geiger state that Christian leaders "should offer training and development for these leaders to help them shepherd their people" (Stetzer and Geiger, 2014, 547–559). We have important lessons to teach the next generation, and we must patiently care for and instruct them. Church leaders who invest time and resources, encourage small-group leaders through coaching relationships, and equip future leaders typically have thriving groups (Egli and Marable, 2014, II). All leaders should similarly value and prioritize guiding the next generation of leaders. We will not only encourage and equip our leaders but also bless the people in their care. Investing in leaders takes more time than a hasty sendoff but strengthens the body of Christ in the long run.

Because multiplication begins when qualified leaders step forward to launch a new group, the shepherd-leader should first look within the group to find an emerging leader or invite a prospective leader into the group. We don't wait for the group members to take the initiative; we take the responsibility to invite them to the table as secondary leaders or apprentices. A shepherd-leader recognizes the potential in an emerging leader and encourages that next generation leader to take ownership. The pathway will look different based on the context, but clearly multiplying leaders affirm the giftedness of others and help them use those gifts. To help them use their spiritual gifts, we must seek God's direction and his plan for their lives.

Persistent in Prayer

Because we're seeking God's direction, protection, and provision, multiplying leaders are praying leaders. One of the most important ways that leaders can shepherd others is through prayer. In their 2014 work, *Small Groups, Big Impact*, Jim Egli and Dwight Marable researched several attributes of healthy, multiplying groups and leaders. They concluded that a leader's prayer life directly impacts the spiritual and numerical growth of his small group. They further explained that praying leaders end up leading groups that are "outward focused...mobilize new leadership...and have a strong impact on the evangelistic effectiveness of the group" (Egli and Marable, 2014, II). Praying leaders shepherd their group in God's might and God provides the increase.

Additionally, prayer is one of our primary weapons to fortify leaders against the attacks of Satan and his evil forces. Evil forces know that if they can cause a leader to fall, all who follow them will be impacted. Only a cruel leader would send someone out the door without proper spiritual armor or continued assistance against the work of a clever and prowling enemy (1 Pet 5:8). Lawless continues to share several ways that Satan aims his strategies particularly at Christian leaders. One of the first is goading leaders to live in self-reliance: "Creativity and strategizing trump prayerful dependence on God...and the enemy relaxes in glee" (Cook and Lawless, 2019). Multiplying leaders want the power of God in their work and turn to him for their strength. They will see

God produce fruit and protect his children against the Evil One as much as they work in the Spirit.

Trusting Delegators

Many leaders will not replicate their ministry because they are too distrusting of their people. One can typically observe a correlation between trust and healthy multiplication. When leaders believe they are the only ones capable of exercising influence or utilizing resources, others will never get the chance to advance in God's kingdom.

The late Eugene Peterson told a candid story of when he faced a breaking point in his ministry. He was overextending himself and managing so many aspects over his growing church that he could not fully focus on prayer, administrating worship, or preaching. He told his elders that he needed to resign because he could not keep doing things this way. He wanted to slow down and focus on pastoring but felt that no one else could fulfill those responsibilities. One interchange with his elders allowed Peterson to recognize the root of his problems.

"'Why don't you let us run the church?'" This was Craig again.

'Because you don't know how.'

Mildred was less than tactful. 'It sounds to me like you aren't doing such a good job yourself. Maybe we could learn.'

They did. And I did.

Instead of a resignation that night, we had a reorganization. We spent the next hour discussing how to go about this. When the evening was over, they had taken over running the church. They assured me they could handle this. All of them said they had learned the running-the-church aspects in their own jobs, professions, and careers—on the job. Each in his or her own way said, 'Trust us'" (Peterson, 2011).

Peterson thought that no one could handle the job like he. Ironically, he was not able to handle the job well himself. If Peterson held tightly onto the leadership reigns, his church could not move forward. He withheld opportunities for developing leaders while also struggling to manage the work himself. I appreciate his candid spirit and the candid response of his leadership team.

Disciples cannot develop for the kingdom or impact the world for Christ on the sideline. Leaders who clutch their roles and influence will miss out on God's plan to develop his flock. We must examine our own hearts for signs of insecurity or fear and confess those to the Lord. Multiplying leaders fully trust God's timing and provision and seek to unleash their people in service of God's kingdom.

When house church leaders trust indigenous leaders (people from within their sphere of influence) the church sees a profound multiplying effect. House churches routinely experience exponential multiplication. J.D. Payne says, "When missionaries exhibit missionary faith, the potential for spontaneous expansion of the church is very high" (Payne, 2008, 138). Leaders must be willing to entrust key leadership roles to people from within their cultural context. Multiplying leaders are confident in God's call to equip the flock for ministry, and they eagerly pour into the lives of others who replicate that movement.

Leaders who replicate possess an innate desire for Spirit-led movements to happen within the life of the community itself. They follow the leading of the Holy Spirit and remember that the same Spirit indwells the hearts of the people they serve. Leaders need to keep a watch over their influence and take special care to not dominate their people. Domineering leaders will not likely see a fresh movement of the Spirit under their leadership. They will produce harm and division rather than joyful, fruitful multiplication. Domineering leaders leave little room for the movement of the Spirit or spiritually healthy future generations.

We received our ministry from God's hands, and as good stewards, we need to be able to deposit aspects of our leadership responsibilities to others. We will likely see people struggle and neglect tasks, but we have struggled the same way if we're honest. As we entrust people with ministry, we will witness emerging leaders thrive on such trust and demonstrate dependability. God will receive the glory. Leaders who recognize God's grace in our own lives can patiently delegate and encourage others to discover their fullest potential.

If we want to see a movement of healthy, multiplying leaders in our ministries, we need to strive for the qualities of a multiplying leader. I'm not talking about bold or charismatic personalities, though they can prove useful. Some healthy leaders are charismatic but so are some unhealthy leaders. Consistently healthy, multiplying leaders show the following traits:

1. Spiritually Healthy
2. Mature in the Faith
3. Shepherding Leaders
4. Persistent in Prayer
5. Trusting Delegators

We must lead like Jesus and prioritize people and their development. He shows us how to open our lives to influence others towards his agenda. We must continually open our hearts to his spiritual work as well as cultivate communities where people can thrive in his will. We want to leave a legacy of spiritually healthy people who use their spiritual gifts and do the work that God calls them to do to their maximum capability.

As the leaders go, so goes the next generation. We want the multiplication movement to begin with God's agenda and flow through us. As God works through us and our leadership, we will see unique blessings in the communities we're influencing and flow to the next generation.

Application Questions:

- Are you the same person whether on the platform, in the classroom, and in your living room?
- Which of these five marks need to become more evident in your life?
- What tests your patience the most while shepherding the people in your care?
- If God's Spirit left your current ministry and plans, how much would change?
- How is your current ministry demonstrating a God-sized faith? Where are you so dependent on him that your ministry plans will fail if he does not answer your prayers?
- If someone joins your team or group for a year, will they look more like Jesus at the end of it?
- When was the last time you delegated a meaningful responsibility to someone and trusted them to do it?
- Who in your ministry exhibits some of these attributes? How can you help them cultivate these marks?
- What counts as a "win" in your organization? What do you need to do to cultivate and celebrate these qualities to produce healthier, multiplying leaders?

6

THE MARKS OF MULTIPLYING GROUPS

COMMUNITY FORMS THE SOIL OF MULTIPLICATION

"Now to him who is able to do far more abundantly than all that we ask or think, according to the power at work within us, to him be glory in the church and in Christ Jesus throughout all generations, forever and ever. Amen." Ephesians 3:20–21

Alone in Asia

As a Christian life and leadership coach, I regularly connect with clients who live around the globe. In 2021, I had a church leader from SE Asia named Paresh send me a Facebook message wanting to discuss leadership multiplication. I hesitated at first because our family was busily gathering support and preparing to move to North Sarasota to plant Living Hope Church. Paresh eagerly wanted to discuss something happening in his country called disciple-making movements.

He told me that a disciple-making movement (DMM) occurs when disciples exponentially multiply to at least the fourth generation.

He claimed to witness thousands coming to faith in Christ in this movement, thousands of churches starting up, and scores of leaders being trained. He said he wanted me to help as a coaching resource for his personal growth and accountability. I decided to chat with him and see where I could help.

In our first conversation, Paresh shared a convincing testimony of salvation and proclaimed a love for God and the church. He also reported exciting numerical growth and stories of multiplication. The longer we talked, he spoke the most about DMMs, training leaders, multiplying churches, and rapid regional expansion. I asked him to tell me more about his spiritual health and local church fellowship. Who helped keep him accountable in his growth? What did the overall health of these baby churches look like? He had much less to say about those matters.

He then proceeded to tell me that with financial support from the American church, the movement could accelerate further. He invited me to take a mission trip to see the ministry firsthand. I told him politely that our church and family could not help much in those areas at this time. However, I knew a pastor from my seminary who lived in that same country. This pastor has a reputation for planting and leading a healthy network of churches. I offered to connect the two of them. Surely this friend could be a valuable help at least for Christian fellowship to a fellow pastor.

Paresh scoffed. He insisted that this pastor would not understand his needs culturally or even care to get to know him due to regional differences. Not being familiar with the regional differences, I did not press the matter. I told him, "I'll be glad to offer leadership coaching and prayer, but you will benefit so much more by connecting in person with the body of Christ."

Paresh and I spoke virtually around five times. I could feel my encouragement to establish healthier patterns of spiritual health and discipleship falling on deaf ears. One day, I opened the social media message board we used for communication and found that he cut me off. My nagging concerns were justified. Paresh did not seem to recognize the value of Christian community.

I've heard from missionaries in areas of the globe with similar concerns about DMMs just like this. Zealous leaders chase visions of rapid expansion and see some success, but at the cost of self-sustaining churches, healthy faith communities, and healthy leaders. What is the point of planting a glut of seeds if we don't water or nurture them? Christ calls us to lead and multiply out of the strength of healthy group life.

If we truly want to join God in his agenda and see him work fully through us to the next generation, we will value God's people. Paul tells us in Ephesians 3 that God will receive glory in his bride, the church. He loves and cares for us, so he created the church for relationship and intimacy. As we pursue God's design to make disciples, we will empower disciples to become disciple-making disciples. Strong Christian community forms the soil for lasting fruit and multiplication for generations.

Strong Communities Bear Lasting Fruit

Developing people to their fullest capability occurs in a team setting. Christ says that he called people together under his kingship to be one body consisting of many parts (1 Cor 12:12–27). No body part is more important or necessary than any other part. Also, no part can function properly apart from the whole. Whether in times of suffering or need, God uses his people to show us his grace. He likewise uses us to help others in their deficits. God does not care merely about the fact that we multiply leaders. He equally cares about *how* and *why* we multiply leaders.

The number of New Testament letters instructing local churches to emphasize the one another ministry shows us what Jesus values. People are his prize. Scripture commands us many times to love, serve, and edify one another. As we build each other up, we will recognize potential leaders and send them out. We will multiply leaders to be bridges for timely needs and help more people. The soil of our leadership development will impact how well our replicated leaders serve the next generation.

The Acts of the Apostles shows how Jesus used his ragtag group of disciples to launch a movement taking the gospel to the nations. Dependent on the Spirit of God and partnering together, they went out into the streets and preached Christ. Thousands turned to the Savior and joined the church. The early church set an incredible model of healthy community. Acts 2:42–47 describes the ongoing activities of the Jerusalem church. While studying the Word and evangelizing, they served Christ together. A unified Christian community demonstrated the power of God and multiplied faith communities all around the world.

Christian community has immense value in multiplication, and I encourage you to cultivate these marks of multiplying groups in your sphere of influence. You can help lead your groups towards these qualities as you clearly communicate the vision. Experts have identified five benchmarks of groups or churches who multiply.

1. Clear on a Vision To Multiply
2. Clear on the Need for Gospel Advancement
3. Relational in Evangelism
4. Knowledgeable of Their Context
5. Committed To Minister as a Group

Clear on a Vision To Multiply

Nothing slows down the effectiveness of a mission like a hazy vision. Before you can multiply groups or leaders, your people must understand the vision. Without a Spirit-led vision for God's plan to develop and multiply people, the movement will inevitably fail. Boren and Egli state, "Long-term success is going to take diligence, humility, and seeking God…if God has put a clear vision for a thriving small group ministry in your heart, you can see it come to fruition as you persist and continue to invite his Spirit" (Boren and Egli, 2014, 64). Leaders must own and promote this vision for their group and to the new people who join the fold.

If we don't communicate the vision frequently, we cannot blame the group for not embracing it. Be wary of forced multiplication. You cannot rush the process of delivering a new baby nor can you rush the birth of a new group. The process of multiplying groups results from effective discipleship. God will grow you and use you to help your people understand the process, learn from your mistakes, and strengthen your focus. As you continue to gain buy-in from your group, you can continually train new leaders, gather core groups, and send them out.

Surratt proposes that when a new group starts, leaders should refresh the established and new groups on the vision. He says, "We should celebrate when a new leader is developed, and a new small group is birthed out of ours. It will be an adjustment to send off a leader who has become an integral part of the group, so the group members need to be reminded of the 'why' behind multiplying" (Surratt, 2019, 142). Keep the vision before the people so that they will likewise share the desire to multiply. Once they share the vision, they will spur us on to be faithful to our calling.

Clear on the Need for Gospel Advancement

Groups that multiply successfully through evangelism and outreach do not stumble into that conclusion. Established churches and groups tend to lose their fervor for outreach, and typically this stagnation occurs as soon as the ten-year mark (Sanchez and Terry, 2015, 411). When groups recognize the urgent need to advance the cause of Christ, they will take intentional and routine steps to address such needs.

Church planting in unchurched areas is one example of addressing the spiritual lostness. The late New York City church planter and pastor Tim Keller noted that new plants "reach more sections of the community, impact new segments of the population, and equip believers for ministry" (Timothy Keller, 2002). Planting leaders and members who study the demographics develop a heart for the community and take intentional steps to evangelize will reach new people. New believers can grow to become new servant leaders for Jesus Christ.

Similar to a church plant's strategy to engage new people for Christ, multiplying groups possess the same intentionality to advance the good news. Several people who possess clarity on the need to multiply can launch a mercy ministry team, seeker friendly group, lunchtime Bible study, or school club for the same purpose. Launching a new group in a new location opens a new avenue for people to access gospel-centered communities. We don't wait for people to come to church on Sunday to find out about Jesus. We go where the needs are.

Strategic intentionality helps the group persevere despite hardships and sacrifices that accompany change. They remember their purpose even through the difficulties of change. Multipliers recognize that multiplying a core group into two groups by necessity requires sending out gifted laborers and embracing new dynamics in those groups. Each new group will have its own DNA, location, group dynamic, and potential. Kingdom advancement still excites the group and motivates them to stretch past those discomforts. The multiplying group may face seasons of setback and revitalization, but they will not abandon the vision. They find fulfillment in emptying themselves of their plans and joining God in his agenda to multiply healthy Christian leaders and groups of disciples.

Because some churches and groups today are truly growing, some Christian leaders may think that a continual push to replicate groups is unnecessary. Unfortunately, many of them grow by shuffling Christians around (Comer, 2014) instead of by evangelizing. Tragically, in a sample Lifeway Research took from 1,000 Southern Baptist churches, only "6.5–7 percent of all churches claimed to grow through conversions" (Rainer, 2017). Thom Rainer analyzed the previously cited Lifeway results and posited, "Evangelism does not happen unless the church is intentional about it" (Rainer, 2017). The lost will not come to Jesus unless someone tells them the gospel (Rom 10:14). The church cannot develop a new generation of leaders merely through church shuffling. We continually need a fresh intake of people to nurture and equip.

Relational in Evangelism

In a survey of missional house churches in the United States of America, church multiplication expert J.D. Payne uncovered an exponential rate of multiplication (Payne, 2008). The thirty-three house churches Payne's team surveyed planted an average of four to six new churches. In just over three years, these daughter churches planted approximately 132 to 198 churches. The multiplication legacy they leave is staggering.

One of the benchmarks for these multiplying house churches was the practice of relational evangelism. These churches prioritized evangelism in their weekly rhythms as opposed to formalized training. Payne says, "Most of these churches reached people with the gospel primarily through the relationships that God had allowed to develop between church members and those who were unbelievers" (Payne, 2008, 96). Rather than hosting large events, these multiplying groups cultivated relationships for the purpose of evangelism using conversations, meals, and other daily activities. They encouraged the flock to meet unbelievers where they were. A multiplying group values every-member evangelism and taking the good news of Jesus Christ into workplaces, schools, and community gatherings.

Pastor and author Robby Gallaty lists one of the marks of a healthy, multiplying small group as relational evangelism, which he associates with "missional living" (Gallaty, 2015, 188). He says, "Missional living happens when group participants are held accountable to build intentional friendships and engage in life-style evangelism" (Gallaty, 2015, 188). Small groups provide helpful avenues for conversations about evangelism and life change. We leaders need accountability and so do our people. As group members grow in evangelism, the group more likely will grow numerically and will need to start new groups.

In Sam Chan's work *Evangelism in a Skeptical World*, he describes the change in Western thinking from modernity to postmodernity—a change that affects relational evangelism. He explains that people are not necessarily looking for what is true but for what works in their daily lives (Chan, 2018, 116). Unbelievers are looking for someone who walks a genuine Christian life, and that can only happen in authentic relationships.

Chan says, "While the gospel is something we speak, words that communicate God's truth, there is also a sense in which we ourselves are a component of how the message is communicated. We speak the words of truth, but we speak the truth in love (Eph. 4:15). Our message is embodied. It doesn't come in a vacuum. It comes in the context of shared lives and trusted friendships" (Sam Chan, 2018, 116). Multiplying groups love God and each other, and the world takes notice. These groups not only share the gospel but also want to get a better grasp of the concerns and problems facing the people they reach.

Knowledgeable of Their Context

Followers of Jesus Christ should view their community and context as their mission field (Matt 9:36). Because developing multiplying communities of disciples is a highly relational task, evangelism and discipleship require getting to know people. Missional groups are eager students of their community and the spiritual needs of the people. We must not rush onto the scene without knowledge because we can mistakenly thrust our own agenda onto people.

Jay Akkerman and Mark Maddix warn in *Missional Discipleship*, "If we are to be good news, we need to listen to the needs and dreams of our surrounding contexts. If we fail to listen, we run the very real risk of placing our own agendas upon the community, rather than seeking to discover what God is already doing in our midst" (Akkerman and Maddix, 2013, 64). Aggressive agendas, no matter how well-intentioned, will cause a disconnect with our hearers, and we can miss an opportunity to effectively share Christ.

Healthy groups do not swing the Bible around like a hammer, hitting anything that moves. Rather, they approach their neighbors' needs like a surgical team armed with scalpels. They prayerfully prepare, patiently understand the symptoms, question the patients, confirm the diagnoses, and meet the deepest needs with truth and grace.

Solid cultural exegesis allows Christian leaders to carry out their mission more effectively outreach and equip their people. When people recognize that you care about them, you will find more opportunities to reach and develop them. In meeting the needs of a few, the group can find their strategy for multiplication and identify leaders qualified for the task at hand.

Committed To Minister as a Group

We've all been a part of a group or church where eighty percent of the people watch twenty percent of the people do all the ministry. One of the most significant attributes of a multiplying group is its emphasis on every member stepping up to serve. Too often believers sit on the sidelines and allow the gifted few to lead. Church leaders need to understand that the most powerful movements of God happen when he moves throughout his people.

Jesus did not keep his disciples on the sidelines of ministry until they understood all things and became Spirit-filled. He discipled them by teaching and service. Today, the underground Chinese churches serve as prime examples of lay ministers leading the way towards multiplication. China had no known house churches in 1949, when Mao Zedong and the Communist Party established their government. Voice of the Martyrs says now, however, "about 130 million Chinese are Christians, most of whom worship within the house church movement" (Global Prayer Guide, 2023).

The Chinese church growth exploded without formal seminary training or in some cases, even a copy of the Bible in the church.

As a persecuted church, the Chinese church also faces a continual leadership deficit because the church leaders or Bible teachers often get arrested (Kuo, 2019). As a result, they encourage all members to help in various aspects of group life and mission. Towns describes how the Chinese church typically addresses teaching needs by immediately enlisting newly converted men to serve in leadership roles. He says, "Every time a [Chinese] man is converted, he is told to come to the house church meeting prepared to speak and/or teach the Word of God" (Towns, 2014, II). The Chinese church must have someone ready to lead even if they are young in the faith. Can you imagine that kind of trust and faith in the Western church?

Learning from the Chinese church, Christian leaders should willingly equip their entire group to serve. God's movement cannot hinge on the gifted few. He works through his imperfect disciples every day. We must call our entire group to use their gifts for the good of others and the glory of God (Ps 90:12; Jas 4:14; 1 Pet 4:10). A group that embraces the kingdom potential in each member's life moves one step closer to multiplication.

The simple nature of multiplication is tied to divestment. If one group or leader clutches onto his or her personal involvement in all aspects of group life, fewer members will develop, and the group cannot multiply. Group leaders must create space where others can step up and contribute. Individuals have limitations in their time, abilities, relationships, and gifting. Together, we can do more for the kingdom. Multiplication can occur when people see God work powerfully in and through the lives of any believer, not just the key leader.

Putting the Pieces Together

I hope that you are encouraged that we can pursue God's plan for multiplication better together. We need to stop trying to fly solo. God's sovereign agenda to fill the earth with disciples and leaders is moving forward through his people. Armed with better awareness of the kind of qualities multiplying leaders and groups possess, I pray the Lord can give you wisdom to find your place in his movement. By God's grace, he can use us Christian leaders to develop the next generation of leaders and cultivate groups with soil for multiplication. One leader can do a lot of good. Healthy teams can do so much more in the long-term: reproducing healthy leaders, teams, and organizations. In the next chapter, I will offer you some concrete steps and practical examples to help you start your multiplication journey.

Application Questions:

- Do you regularly gather with other believers for discipleship and fellowship? Do you tend to serve the Lord solo or recruit others to help you on mission?
- Who is helping encourage and mentor you in the faith? How are you spurring others on in their intimacy with Christ and obedience to him?
- Do you know your group's purpose and mission? What is your vision to help accomplish that mission? Can your people articulate the mission and vision back to you?
- Would you describe your group culture as comfortable or missional? How can you use your God-given influence to help them get back or stay on God's agenda?

- How do you encourage your family, church, or group to reach new people for Christ outside their Christian circle? What does effective outreach look like in your context?
- What does your feedback loop look like? Who has permission to come speak candidly about your mistakes or indecision? How do you respond when confronted?
- What trainings or resources do you provide to help sharpen your team to the best of their abilities?

7

MAKING PROGRESS

PRACTICAL STEPS TO START MULTIPLYING TODAY

Jesus the Master modeled disciple-making and leadership development so well in the New Testament. Today, we imperfect disciples still struggle to grasp how to get that done in our sphere of influence. Especially if we've never observed a leader in our field replicate their leadership. To make matters more challenging, many churches and groups do not have systems in place to further that mission. Churches tend to look to outside hires to come and get things moving for them.

God clearly directed you to this resource for a reason. Cultures and systems take time to build, but leaders use their influence to get the group moving. It's time for all of us to take the pieces Christ has handed us and get to work investing in his people.

You may need to overcome some mental obstacles. "I'd like to start doing that in a few years, but I need to hire someone first." "We need to restructure our ministry before we can really develop people." Perhaps you're trying to address symptoms without utilizing the heartbeat of the Great Commission: reaching, winning, building, and sending disciples of Jesus Christ.

If developing leaders remains only an idealistic thought for you, the gap will remain. You can start right now by building up the person next to you or underneath your care. I'll share how the development process can look at every level of the ordinary Christian leader's sphere of influence. First, we need to understand the pathway to get a pupil to the level of mentor leader.

The Pathway from Pupil to Mentor

My oldest two sons just recently started their martial arts journey. It's brand new to me as I've mostly been an organized team sports guy. What I do know is that beginners start with white belts and advance their way up the ranks in hopes of earning the coveted black belt. It was impressive to witness the instructors do a fantastic job helping the young ones learn and have fun at their first session. At the same time, they kept telling the students, "This is a black-belt school. We do everything with excellence." They prepare the youngest students for the journey towards the black belt from day one.

The journey for a mentor to guide a pupil to a mastery level takes intentionality and persistence. As we do not have belt rankings in Christian ministry, a helpful pathway for developing Christian disciples and leaders typically has these four steps.

Step 1 — I do. You watch.

Teaching and demonstration form the bulk of this initial phase. The pupil observes the mentor.

Step 2 — I do. You help.

Experiential learning plays a pivotal role. The pupil joins on mission and helps with the mentor's work and community life.

Step 3 — You do. I help.

The mentor begins to transfer specific leadership responsibilities to the pupil and evaluates his or her progress. Together, they identify potential stressors and weaknesses.

Step 4 — You do. I watch.

The pupil obtains a form of mastery. The mentor delegates authority and allows the pupil to lead. The mentor then takes on the role of a coach.

Overall, this pathway works well to turn one leader into two. Every step is vital for effective leadership multiplication, and teachable learners and intentional mentors are necessary to the process. Many leaders struggle to guide their pupils to level four. To make a biblical disciple, remember your pupil must be able to one day reach, win, build, and send disciples. When we train leaders, we haven't fully replicated our leadership until we can walk away and entrust our protegee to carry the baton in our absence. We can check on them later for coaching and encouragement, but we must prepare the next generation to lead in our physical absence.

Multiplication at Every Level

A leader can initiate replication in several areas at once. If you lead from the top, you cannot invest in everyone equally nor should you. God calls you to build a culture where every Christian leader can thrive and multiply for Christ. I'll focus on three spheres of personal influence: the individual, the team, and the multi-layered organization.

Start with One

One pastor found a future elder in this unusual way. He stared disheartened at a badly cluttered closet in the church building. Years of neglect and people dumping unwanted items led to a mess that nobody cared to address. The pastor knew the church needed someone to clean it up, and he probably needed to do it himself. He also wanted to spend time investing in someone else. He made an announcement to the church that he was going to clean that closet on the next Saturday morning and invited others to help him. On the following Saturday morning, only one man showed up. Still, the pastor and that one volunteer spent several hours cleaning and talking. They continued to develop the relationship over time. Gradually, the pastor began to disciple and offer leadership opportunities to this man. He led humbly and well. The pastor entrusted more and more responsibilities to him. Eventually, the church recognized the clear work of God on this thriving man and ordained him to the church elder team. Who would have expected such a beautiful gift to come from a disorganized closet? Praise God for bringing a mindful pastor and a willing helper together.

You can make a significant impact investing in one teachable pupil. If you know a Christian who expresses willingness to serve Jesus with his or her gifts, seek out an opportunity to mentor them in leadership. Since disciple-making and development requires proximity, I recommend choosing an individual of the same gender.

Initiate the conversation. Express your desire to invest in them and what that could look like. If you've previously neglected helping them, you may need to apologize for not taking the initiative before. Let them know that their development is truly a priority for you. Schedule time for one-on-one meetings or even a lunch where they can have space to talk, and you can listen. Some sample questions for an exploratory one-on-one include the following:

- What do you enjoy most about your service here?
- Do you feel as if we're successfully accomplishing our mission? Why or why not?
- What is the most fulfilling part of your role?
- What challenges do you experience? What would you do to address those issues?
- Where would you like to grow with your gifts and opportunities this next year?
- Where do you see yourself serving the Lord in five years?

As this prospective leader opens up, listen carefully. Pray in the Spirit and ask God to help you discern where he wants you to help them. Critically evaluate how you can help them. Depending on the sphere of influence, your expertise, or their immediate needs, step one can take a different shape. Beginning with a Bible study is often effective, so you can have fuel for the soul and clarity on God's will. As the two of you grow, you can discuss and pursue contextualized application for steps 2–4 of the pathway.

If you cannot think of a particular person to start mentoring, that is not abnormal. I remember one time one of my good pastor friends asked me to help him start a new small group in our church. I laughed and brushed him off! (In my defense, I thought he was joking). Thankfully, he brought it up again a second time, and I was able to prayerfully discern that the Lord's hand was at work here. During the next two years, we saw disciples made and marriages strengthened. We also intentionally equipped three men in the group to be able to lead. To this day, those leaders are still serving as examples of Christian leaders whether as Bible study leaders or deacons. I recently saw that one of them started another new group within that church. Praise God for bringing fruit when I didn't even have vision to see it!

Where can you stir the water so that a potential leader can surface? Look first to some of the pressing needs in your ministry. As the Lord leads, take responsibility to address that need with the help of a servant leader. Patiently guide that helper down the replication pathway. You will not only empower a new leader but also develop a culture of replication and investment.

Small-Group Explosion

Several years ago, I recognized that my physical health needed to become a greater priority in my life. My brother recommended I join his early morning workout group. The only problem is they meet at 5:15 a.m. on Wednesday mornings. Outdoors. Rain or shine. In a parking lot.

I have no rational idea for why I went, but I felt compelled to check it out. I showed up for a workout, but I left with lessons about life, leadership, and multiplication. I also left with the nickname "Sparkler," and if you're a man who ever shows up for a beatdown in the "gloom" (pre-workout gathering) in F3 Suncoast, I'll be glad to tell you why.

We're called F3. F3 is a national network of free, peer-led workouts for men. We plant, grow, and serve these groups to invigorate male community leadership. The three F's stand for Fitness, Fellowship, and Faith. Though not a Christian organization, numerous Christians participate in the weekly workouts. F3 provides an excellent model of multiplication and leadership development for volunteers. Started in 2011, some men in Charlotte, North Carolina hosted a free workout open to all men. Now boasting an astonishing 4,300 workouts around the globe, F3 is a life-changing movement that helps me become physically fit and find brotherly fellowship.

One of the things that sets F3 apart is that each beatdown is led by volunteer peers in a rotating fashion. We have regional and site leaders, but volunteers drive everything. From the beginning, members invite men of all backgrounds and physical regimens to step out of their comfort zone and lead. Developing men into virtuous leaders is not just a part of the mission, it **is** the mission.

The men who materialize in the gloom each week are urged to show up and spur each other onto to pursue something bigger than ourselves. Each week the "Q," (rotating leader), presents the mission and core principles to the group. He creates the workout and accepts the responsibility to make sure it is well planned and articulated. No man is left behind. Often, what starts as a 45-minute or hour-long workout turns into a leader development masterclass. The Q does this in several ways:

- Count in Cadence—Counting in cadence requires the group to be in lockstep during the exercises and take ownership of the group's progress.
- Enlist Co-Leaders—The Q often spreads the group into sub-groups and enlists volunteers to guide their peers through the round of exercises.
- Leadership Reps—Sometimes a Q will give leadership reps to other men. We call this the "round of Mary," where a man from the circle must choose his favorite exercise and lead the group in a ten count of that movement.

Once an F3 man gets a firm grasp on the mission and flow of our beatdowns, we will challenge him to sign up to lead his first beatdown. We call this the "VQ," and it's a big deal in F3 Nation. Experienced members offer guidance for putting together an excellent workout. Men from all over the region show up in strong numbers to support the new Q.

These newbies do not lead because they're the best physical specimens we have (hey, just look at me!). We encourage them to lead so they can grow and serve. They might stumble through their explanations at times and need some help counting or adapting the exercises. At all times the group builds them up, participates in the workout, and offers praise and feedback at the end. As men see a need for a new beatdown in a new area, they recruit others, cast the vision, and take the responsibility to launch it. New groups reach new men, and the process starts all over.

You can see how F3 has exploded so quickly. If a non-Christian organization can believe so heavily in the personal development of the next generation of leaders, why can't the body of Christ? Bodily exercise profits some, but spiritual growth benefits even more (1 Tim 4:8).

What principles and practices can you begin in your group? Your staff? Where can you give your team members some reps and feedback? Here are some easy starting points:

- Preparing and Sharing Devotionals
- Leading in Prayer
- Appoint Someone To Handle Communications with the Team
- Create Sub-groups and Group Leaders for Projects
- Leading Discussions on Values and Goals
- Celebrating Team Wins
- Enabling your Team To Select the Next Priority or Outreach

Your team will gradually increase in their ability to lead at a higher capacity. You can foster a culture where everyone can be bridge builders outside of the staff meeting and continue the people's development. You might face some people on your team who refuse to get on board. You could look to outside resources (coaches, consultants, fellow leaders, or networks) to help you love and lead these difficult people well.

Multi-Layered Organization

For those gifted to oversee multiple layers of leadership in a non-profit, you face greater complexities. You have established cultures, numerous personalities, and organizational interdependence. Unity is key, and the Spirit must lead you in the application of this calling. Your road will need to be well laid out, so think carefully about the long-term path. I highly recommend the book *Building Leaders: Blueprints for Developing Leadership at Every Level of Your Church*. Aubrey Malphurs and Will Mancini masterfully propose the process for holistically building this kind of culture. For the purposes of this book, I recommend the simple progression below.

Step 1: Set the Example

Clearly, you must demonstrate healthy, multiplying leadership while you cast the vision to others. Start with replication individually as described in The Pathway from Pupil to Mentor. If you don't invest, don't expect others to tithe their precious time to invest in the next generation.

Step 2: Gather Support

Recruit the support of your teams (staff, partners, deacons, key leaders, etc.). Use your influence to build bridges to people in key leadership positions. Make sure you listen well for buy-in and support. Take your time to communicate clearly and often. You might take them through a book study on multiplying leadership. Do not merely send an email and assume that everyone is on the same page as you. Also, look at your budget and ensure you have the resources to develop leaders well. If you struggle to gather momentum in any of these areas, I highly recommend you seek out an outside coach or consultant to help you address the challenges.

Step 3: Identify Leadership Levels

In *Building Leaders*, Aubrey Malphurs and Will Mancini give an excellent delineation of leaders in a church that involves small-group leaders and coaches (Malphurs and Mancini, 21). They list six levels of leadership. You can examine if you have this kind of build-out capability in your organization or what levels you need.

1. Apprentice Group Leaders
2. Group Leaders
3. Apprentice Coaches
4. Coaches
5. Ministry Staff and Pastoral Staff
6. Elders

Now you should map out the levels of leadership in your church or organization. No matter how many levels you have, each level should know how to replicate healthy disciples and leaders. Is it clear to everyone and not just you? Does everyone understand his or her role? Who takes responsibility for equipping each of the levels? We need to take special care to keep both volunteers and staff on the same page. The bigger your organization, the more often you need to communicate and refine the vision for your people.

Step 4: Training Strategy

How can you equip leaders at every level with the right tools, mentoring, and support to succeed? If you keep mentoring and discipling as the heartbeat for your strategy, you have the essentials. Jesus replicates healthy Christian leaders by his Word, and he leads his people by the Spirit to do so. We must build rhythms where we can regularly inform, unify, encourage, and develop our teams. Most leaders enjoy taking advantage of coaching, training, and conferences. Wouldn't we want our people to receive some of those same benefits? Here are some ideas to implement:

- Leadership Coaching (Monthly)
- Leadership Training Events in House (Biannually)
- Team Retreats (Annually)
- Appreciation or Celebration with Families Included (Annually)
- Themed Conferences (Every other year)

I love providing resources for my people. I have so many good memories with our leaders around a dinner table, learning in a workshop, or attending a conference together. A few years back, I found a Youth Pastor Summit in Nashville. I wanted to give some of my leaders the opportunity to learn about reaching the next generation alongside my wife and me. I invited some staff and student leaders and booked an Airbnb for the trip. We had thirteen leaders join us for that three-day trip. We took the 16-hour round trip from Raleigh in two of our church's old fifteen passenger vans and had some unforgettable adventures along the way. On the way back home, we had tires start to give out on the highway, which led to an 8-hour long process finding the right tires to replace. We then drove through the night arriving back at 4 a.m.! We were exhausted but thankful. We loved each other, and we were unified in the work God called us to do.

My greatest joy was witnessing the leaders worship and devour the Word. They took notes, workshopped ideas over lunch, and critiqued speakers according to the Word. I was so fired up for them and for our ministry. We not only grew close to those leaders but also got a front-row seat to God pouring into this next generation of leaders. Out of that group, two of them now serve as student pastors. The entire group served our students well and continue to serve as Christian leaders to this day. I can't take credit for any of that. God used me to open an opportunity for them to pursue and cultivate their calling and gifts.

A Worthwhile Investment

Invest in your people the way you want someone to invest in you. Watch what God does as your people grasp the vision. They will flourish in your organization and serve your community needs. Going deeper with your people will lead to long-lasting and far-reaching fruit. You may see more healthy churches. You might witness your non-profit expand operations. You might start new ministries to serve a new demographic in your community. You may start new small groups to disciple more people. Christian businesses may expand to share Christian values and exceptional service to the community. Christian counselors may help more people address the deep issues of hurting hearts. You never know what God can do but give these people your best and watch them give their best for the King.

Focused training strategies will cost you time and money. However, if God calls us to prioritize our people, then he is good for the reward. Jesus sent his disciples out with a joyful heart. He gave them the fullest investment through his Spirit, Word, and example.

Let's follow the Lord's example and invest deeply in our people so that they can grow in Christ. The next generation will benefit. Whatever it takes, even our very lives, this investment will be worth it. For all of eternity we will celebrate Jesus's sacrifice for us (Rev 5:9) in giving his all to turn his enemies into his bride. We can easily give our resources to show his glory and serve others.

8

ANSWERING THE CLARION CALL
OUR COMMITMENT TO MOVING FORWARD TOGETHER

I pray that as the clarion call sounds for healthier, multiplying leaders, you find your place to fill the gap. If you're ready to reevaluate your "business as usual" and step onto the Father's agenda, God will connect with you other like-minded believers. We recognize the movement to multiply healthy leaders will cut across the grain of the status quo and will require a collective partnership from believers around the world. I've seen unlikely partnerships turn into beautiful partnership in various ministry fields. Standing alongside other believers on mission will help us go farther in the long haul. Leaders especially need helpful resources, collaboration, and ongoing development. Sharp leaders who intentionally partner with other Christian leaders for the kingdom become catalysts for leadership multiplication.

Most Valuable Servants

One of my favorite parables from Jesus is the Parable of the Talents (Matt 25:14–30; Luke 19:12–27). Jesus told his disciples that God gives each disciple certain gifts. In the story, the Master bestows many gifts. Some servants have more talents than others. Those that steward their gifts well, the Master blesses. Even if you only have one gift, Jesus does not love or bless you any less. He blesses according to how we invest what he gave us.

To be clear, God does not guarantee that anyone will have a rapidly growing ministry or scores of leaders. We are accountable to Christ for how we use (or neglect) what gifts we use. Everything in our lives ultimately belongs to his lordship. We must cultivate and invest to our fullest capabilities. If we want to be healthy, multiplying leaders for the long haul, we need to invest in our personal enrichment.

Sharpening the Axe

Abraham Lincoln is widely attributed as saying, "Give me six hours to chop down a tree and I will spend the first four sharpening the axe." A sharp instrument is the best way to ensure a job is done right. Leaders should continually sharpen our minds and hone our capabilities if we are to lead others towards God's vision. Sharp leaders are the tip of the axe cutting through obstacles and equipping others to make disciples of Christ and step up as leaders. We want to be sharp instruments who are useful in the hands of our King. He deserves our best and so do our people. Some of the ways we can sharpen ourselves for long term:

- Read and learn (books and podcasts on Christian living, doctrine, history, leadership biographies, poetry, fiction, etc.).
- Block space in our calendar for reflection and writing.
- Pick up an exercise regimen (lifting, cycling, boxing, MMA) that challenges you and keeps you fit.

- Audit or enroll in seminary or business school classes (a quality education costs something so count the cost).
- Pursue certification that enhances your skillset (coaching, marketing, finance, project management).
- Write a book (discipline yourself to put thought to pen and share a message with others).
- Instruct other in a classroom or workshop

I never dreamt of pursuing advanced education earlier in life. To me, spending more time in the classroom was a chore and unnecessary. Of course, as the Lord called me to step up in pastoral leadership, I knew I needed sharpening. Once I started taking seminary classes, I realized that I needed it even more. I grew up in church, but my knowledge of the doctrine and the ministry of the Word needed sharpening. I fell more in love with Jesus as I studied his Word in the original languages and learned about how to help other people follow him. My professors passed on hundreds of collective years in research, knowledge, and experience. As Proverbs 27:17 says, "Iron sharpens iron." For years, some of the sharpest irons guided my mind immensely. I also grew to value peer to peer cohorts where colleagues can critique my assumptions and expand my thinking and encourage me to write further on helpful topics.

I do not share my story assuming you also need a seminary education. You might not and I don't want to add unnecessary debt to your shoulders. The point is that we all need to pursue a lifetime of learning and sharpening from others. For those working in business leadership or finance, you might pursue an MBA or join a local business leaders' group. You might elect further training through specific certifications or licensing. Your budget may prohibit you from taking some traditional educational paths but do not let that limit your overall development. My wife and I chose to become certified Christian coaches and found so much benefit in our overall skills and conversations. We became better listeners in our marriage and ministry. God opened doors to put those skills to use immediately helping others. When you allow God to sharpen you to the most profitable instrument possible, he will give you opportunities to invest in the next generation of leaders.

Opening the Sails

Be careful when you open your sails because you never know where God will take you. At the start of 2020, God stirred my heart to become a more skilled leader for my people. My sphere of influence at our church grew to encompass a growing number of leaders, students, and families and I wanted to lead them well. I chose to pursue the advanced degree of Doctor of Ministry at the Southeastern Baptist Theological Seminary.

I started pursuing the doctorate while in the position of Student Pastor. As I progressed through the degree, I was amazed to see how God taught me exactly what I needed to know as our church needed more from me. Unbeknownst to me, COVID-19 would soon rock the world and bring so much change to the ministry landscape. The pressure of leadership increased exponentially through these changes along with emotional and physical exhaustion, decision fatigue, peacemaking efforts, and the added responsibility of overseeing our adult education ministries.

In God's perfect timing, I had access to quality resources, a cohort of brothers, and mentors to help me navigate the increased pressures. SEBTS offered free counseling to students in ministry. I could put the skills learned in conflict reconciliation and strategic leadership to use and help our church tackle complex issues. God gave me what I needed when I needed it.

He continued to provide all that we needed when he called our family to a new mission field in Florida to plant a new gospel-preaching church. Cross-cultural ministry and entrepreneurial leadership is never easy, but my education and experience equipped me to handle those responsibilities. Now, God is calling me to pass this message onto you. What will you do with it now?

Whatever your particular calling, open your sails to continual learning, assessment, and change. Without our previous period of testing and learning, I could not be prepared for this calling today. Every day is God's kingdom serves a purpose. As we trust God's providence, he will guide us towards deeper health and farther influence. You'll never know when or how God will work in your situation but trust his ways and he will bring it to pass.

Leadership Coaching

Leadership coaching helps you unlock the fullest potential for your leadership and organization. I cannot recommend coaching highly enough. Hopefully you already saw the benefit in Exodus 18 when Jethro helped Moses multiply leaders. Moses received Jethro's guidance and found a healthier ministry approach. I know a lot of leaders who see the benefit in attending leadership conferences and reading books. This is a good starting place. Unfortunately, more knowledge does not necessarily lead to more action. Leadership experts can only help you so much from a distanced platform. We benefit much more from someone stepping into our world, understanding our issues, and helping us develop a strategy to move forward.

A personal coach cares about you and can give specialized attention to your needs and ministry. They listen, ask insightful questions, and help you discover new paths around ministry obstacles. With an outsider's perspective, they can spot things that you have become accustomed to overlooking. An experienced coach can also be a sounding board and advise you against unnecessary decisions that lead to long-term issues. The Bible tells us that there is safety in a multitude of counselors (Prov 11:14). Invest some of your conference or book money into a leadership coach. They will more than pay for themselves. You can have access to your coaches through personal communication and monthly meetings. Some of the ways that a coach can help you is:

- Assessing your ministry leadership
- Encouraging you towards spiritual and emotional health
- Building a leadership pipeline
- Creating a multiplying strategy for your groups and leaders
- Helping you develop and cast a vision to your team
- Navigating relational conflicts
- Setting goals and following through

If you secure a leadership coach, you can develop a relationship that has the potential to yield much fruit in the long term. Think of it as investing in yourself. You can only take others as far as you are able to go. Your organization will thank you! No matter the ministry seasons we're in, we always need more insight. No matter how gifted the leader, we all have blind spots and weaknesses. We can become more well-rounded and capable leaders with someone coaching and challenging us.

I am grateful that my church planting network, Send Network Florida, provides monthly coaching to me. I have an experienced and accessible coach named Mark who adds so much value to my life. He cares about me as a person and has proven himself to be a confidential and encouraging sounding board for my ministry. I always come away with a clearer focus and actionable steps.

I would love for every Christian leader to have the same quality access to a leadership coach. For this reason, I started Leader 2 Leader Coaching. As a certified coach and leader, I would happily serve as a catalyst for you to discover and carry out God's agenda. Imagine the scores of healthy, multiplying leaders you can have in your organization. If it is God's will work together to make that happen. Simply visit leader2leadercoaching.com for a free resource and to schedule a free discovery call. Let's see how personal leadership coaching or a coaching cohort can help you get going.

Outside Consultants

Why is it that cars only break down at the least convenient time? It seems, in our family at least, that we always find a dead battery or flat tire when we're in a shopping plaza at night. Our car never fails when we try to start it at home. To lower the frequency of such incidents, we need to pop the hood and check our vehicles from time to time. If you're like me and not too familiar with all the parts of your car, you need a mechanic's keen eye. Don't wait to call the mechanic until you're heading for a breakdown.

Like the many systems of a car, an organization depends on many factors for health and growth. Your ministry or group will not stumble its way toward success. Leaders need to know the importance of checkups, evaluations, and top to bottom evaluations. One of the best ways to evaluate your work is to enlist the help of an outside consultant. A consultant can assess many aspects of your organization health and overall missional effectiveness. They can assist with:

- Running demographic reports on your community and organization
- Measuring the gap between your organization's self-perception and reality
- Understanding God's vision for your people
- Crafting a clear and memorable mission statement
- Recognizing optimal core values for health and growth
- Identifying the next important hires
- Uncovering communication breakdowns
- Recognizing dysfunctional teams and personalities
- Creating new strategies to develop leaders
- Training staff and key leaders

Do not wait too long to ask for help or until you have an organizational breakdown. One consultant from North Carolina told my previous team that most organizations wait to call for help until they are in crisis mode. Obviously, they can help in those situations but now they're helping you react. Wise leadership looks to be proactive.

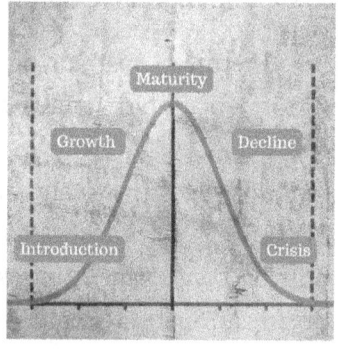

The best time to hire a consultant can be when things are growing well and peaking towards maturity. Looking at the Sigmoid curve to the right, you can see that organizational maturity will turn into decline without the start of a new S curve. At some point what worked in the past loses effectiveness. Remember Blockbuster. Unless you can reassess your strategies and change you will struggle to accomplish your mission in a rapidly changing world. Healthy organizations invite assessments and initiate adjustments early and often. Consultants can help you see where you need to go and help you get there efficiently.

Of course, hiring a consultant will not erase potential problems or dysfunction. Rainer says that a shocking fifty percent of his Church Answer's consultations are ineffective because the churches do not follow through on the recommendations (Rainer, 2024). Many leaders say that they are teachable and open to change, but they refuse to take the hard steps towards growth. If you want to see God unleash a leader replicating movement in your organization, you must be willing to make changes.

Catalysts for the Kingdom

Multiplying leaders not only want to see God move in their organization, but honestly desire for God's fullest agenda to spread all around the globe. Every Christian leader should view themselves as partners with the universal church for the kingdom of God. We should desire for the Word of God to abound and transform many different peoples and communities. To get there, we must check our egos at the door and posture ourselves and our ministries to build bridges to others. Are you trying to build towers or bridges? Bridge builders continually reach out. If we have strong, growing organizations, we especially bear the burden to use our resources to serve and advance others.

Ministry is Global

I had a professor in college who had a heartbeat to serve the nations. He used to say something memorable that I carry with me to this day. "Life is ministry and ministry is global" (Brian Trainer). Every day we get up, God is working through his children to advance his kingdom around the world. We're called to keep the big picture before us in our work and partner with others towards that end. Not only should we partner with believers in a local church and missional groups, but we should look outside of our groups to partner with peer organizations.

Kingdom collaboration is essential to properly carry out the Great Commandments and the Great Commission. Christians struggle at times to genuinely celebrate "wins" and growth in another organization down the road if our own group does not benefit. As we've seen from the Word, multiplying for the Lord is a benefit and reward all on its own. Faithful servants of Jesus Christ serve the same Master. We want *his* kingdom to come, and *his* will to be done on earth as it is in heaven (Matt 6:10). We pray along with our Savior that all believers will be unified in the same Spirit as the Father and Son (John 17:21). In addition to the spiritual blessings, we see so much fruit when we partner together.

For all our flaws, this is the biggest strength of the Southern Baptist Convention of which our church family is a part. Churches partner together to advance the gospel to the farthest reaches of the globe. We've seen fruit in many ways: more missionaries, Christian seminary education, disaster relief response, pro-life advocacy, foster care, and exponential increase in new church plants and planting leaders.

I've witnessed the fruit firsthand in Florida as like-minded churches partner strategically through a network called Send Network Florida. Working as a team with Send Network as our pipeline, we can assess new planters, adopt daughter churches, send out teams, send timely resources, and provide additional support. Churches we never knew existed reached out to us in our planting and asked how they could help Living Hope Church in North Sarasota. We've grown because others saw the vision and gave. By God's grace, we want to be a multiplying church and it will take partnerships like that to see it happen. When one work of God succeeds, we all celebrate. This is healthy multiplication.

Florida Baptist churches currently plant 75 churches around the state each year. In a state that grows by 1,000 people every day, we need more of this ongoing, statewide collaboration. Florida Baptists partner with Southern Baptist churches around the world to fuel global missions. Just this past week I spoke on the phone with a missionary and church leader in eastern Europe. I cannot share his name due to safety concerns, but this millennial serves with the International Mission Board. He answered God's call to serve in medical missions overseas but acknowledged that he needed so much help to get there. The IMB and partnering churches gave him the support he needed and assigned him to a team in the Ukraine. When Russia invaded the Ukraine, the IMB helped his team relocate to a different country in easter Europe. All of this was possible because of God's provision through like-minded partnerships.

I don't share this to brag on Southern Baptists or say that you must be a part of a convention or denomination. I share this so that you rethink the overall purpose of your organization. One Christian sub-group cannot reach everyone. Think carefully about the following questions:

- How can you lead your group to partner with other Christian brothers and sisters down the street?
- What will you do to address the needs of single moms or foster children in your area?
- What portion of your budget is allotted to generosity and kingdom advancement?
- Where has God placed you to bring other leaders to the table to pray and strategize about joining forces for God's worldwide agenda?

Christians who share resources can also better serve the marginalized and underserved peoples. I spoke before about the benefits of F3 in my physical and leadership sharpening. I've also seen F3 men at their best when they partner together to serve the needy. There's something incredible about seeing these strong men make time to feed the homeless, travel on mission trips, or mobilize community members to respond to foster needs and fundraisers. In just my workout group in Sarasota, I've seen men send medical supplies and clothing to needy villagers in Cuba. One brother started a monthly serve night at a local Salvation army so that men can help other men less fortunate than themselves. We're strengthened through sharing life and leadership together and we can develop better pathways to reach and empower the next generation. We will also meet more needs around the world. Do you want to see healthier, multiplying Christian leaders around the globe? Start partnering with the believers next door.

CONCLUSION
MAKE YOUR TIME COUNT

"I've got some exciting news. I wanted to reach out and let you know that I preached my first sermon last night in our student ministry...I've been thinking about the start of this journey and of course wouldn't be here without you and your intentionality in my life (as always carried out by Jesus). Thank you!!"

I read that text this morning from a former student. Before that moment, I was trying to think of some clever hook for this book's conclusion. I cannot describe the deep sense of joy, gratitude, and fulfillment that washed over me as I read his encouraging text. To know that God is calling my former student to step up and preach the Word to the next generation means the world to me. As the Apostle John said, "I have no greater joy than to hear that my children are walking in the truth" (3 John 4). This is our hook. Every Christian leader on the planet can experience moments like this. When you invest your days making disciples and developing leaders, even on the hard days, God will bring about a harvest in due season (Gal 6:9).

How can you use your time to bridge the gap to the next generation? Our clarion call as spiritual leaders in the kingdom of God is not merely to lead but to multiply — to raise up a new generation of godly, influential, and vibrant leaders who will shine Christ's light in every corner of the world. Not only should we do this, but by God's design and grace, we will.

When Jesus returns to set up his eternal kingdom, and the family gathers around the table with him, we will hear story after story of how he used his servants to advance his redemptive plan. Each generation will weave together the tapestry of God's glorious grace. For the good of others and the glory of God. Imagine seeing how the thread of your life intertwined with future generations to contribute to that tapestry.

As we survey the troubling landscape of unhealthy and absentee Christian leaders today, we face a choice. We can continue to prioritize ourselves and limit our focus to the pressing issues of the day. Or we can follow Moses' example, repent for our misplaced priorities, and open the reigns of leadership to others. When we acknowledge our limitations, we look to God's agenda for building the bridge to the next generation and multiplication occurs. Jesus teaches us that making disciples and developing leaders requires proximity to his people and intentional discipleship. If the King of all can entrust his gospel ministry and church to imperfect disciples, we can also propel our mentees to carry the torch to new frontiers.

As we look to become and develop healthy multiplying leaders, we should know that healthy, multiplying leaders who consistently replicate leaders exhibit benchmarks of spiritual health and maturity in the faith. They also take a shepherding approach to develop others, persistently pray, and delegate because they trust their team. Multiplying groups tend to possess a clear vision to multiply and recognize a clear need for gospel advancement. They additionally take a relational approach to evangelism, get to know their context, and commit to ministering as a group. When more Christian leaders and groups embrace this missional mindset, we will see a God-centered movement that outlasts us and goes far beyond what we could have envisioned.

To be clear, we are not in this movement for ourselves. Christ deserves to see the reward for his suffering. Imagine seeing his loving face in heaven and hearing him say, "Well done, good and faithful servant" (Matt 25:23). We will never be more aware of our own unworthiness and the fullness of his grace. His kindness will be more than enough reward for us. To see the scores of lives we helped impact for Christ brings further praise to his name.

Look at people the way that Jesus does. Invest in people the way he does. Seek out an emerging leader and invest the Word and your life into them. Encourage them to use their gifts and cultivate them. Give them reps to learn how to lead well and propel them to appropriate levels of influence in your organization. Hold them accountable and be accountable to them. Cast the vision to your team and group leaders so that they mobilize their group to make an eternal difference.

I've offered some practical guidance to help you assess your current approach to leadership and realign with God's vision for replication. One chapter I could not write for you is the exact strategy or pipeline you are responsible to create. I'm a catalyst who can offer guidance, but God appointed *you* to be the leader who takes responsibility to carry out his vision for your context and community. Trust that God put you there for a reason. Take this resource to help you identify and equip more leaders who are both spiritually healthy and able to replicate their leadership.

Remember that we multiply better by working together. Reach out to other leaders, coaches, or consultants who can offer counsel and guidance on building leadership pipelines and strategies from the top down. Most importantly, let God's Word and Spirit guide you. Open your sails, and he will fill you and use you to invest in the next generation of leaders. King Jesus tells us the time is now. The clarion call has sounded, and we must answer it. We must steward our time well. Let's invest our days wisely so that a new generation of godly, influential, and vibrant leaders will shine Christ's light in every corner of the world.

REFERENCES

Akkerman, J. R. and M. A. Maddix. (2013). *Missional Discipleship: Partners in God's redemptive mission.* Beacon Hill Press.

Alexander, T. D. (2017). *Exodus.* (Apollos Old Testament Commentary). IVP Academic.

Arnold. J. (2004). *The big book on small groups.* IVP Connect.

Ash, C. (2016). *Zeal without burnout: Seven keys to a lifelong ministry of sustainable sacrifice.* The Good Book Co.

Barna, G. (2014). *Today's pastors.*

Barna Group. (Mar 15 2023). *Excerpt: A rapid decline in pastoral security.* https://www.barna.com/research/pastoral-security-confidence/.

Barna Research. (Feb 15 2017). *How healthy are pastors' relationships?.* https://www.barna.com/research/healthy-pastors-relationships/

Blackaby, H. and R. Blackaby (2011). *Spiritual Leadership: Moving people onto God's agenda.* B&H Books.

Blanchard, K., P. Hodges, and P. Hendry. (2016). *Lead like Jesus: Lessons from the greatest leadership role model of all time.* W Publishing.

Boren, M. S. (2014). *Leading small groups in the way of Jesus.* IVP.

Boren, M. S. (2010). *Missional small groups: Becoming a community that makes a difference in the world.* Baker Books.

Boren, M. S. and J. Egli. (2014). *Small group models: Navigating the commonalities and the differences.* (CEJ 11).

Brenan, M. (Jan 10, 2023). *Nurses retain top ethics rating in u.s., but below 2020 high.* (Gallup). https://news.gallup.com/poll/467804/nurses-retain-top-ethics-rating-below-2020-high.aspx.

Carson, D. A. (1991). *The gospel according to John.* IVP; W.B. Eerdmans.

Chan, S. (2018). *Evangelism in a skeptical world: How to make the unbelievable news about Jesus more believable.* Zondervan Academic.

Coleman, R. E. (1964). *The master plan of evangelism.* Fleming H. Revell.

Comiskey, J. (2002). *Home cell group explosion: How your small group can grow and multiply.* Touch Pub.

Crawford, B. (2022). *The crisis of vacant pulpits.* Baptist Bulletin. https://baptistbulletin.org/the-baptist-bulletin-magazine/the-crisis-of-vacant-pulpits/.

Downen, R., L. Olsen, and J. Tedesco. (2019). *Abuse of faith.* (Houston Chronicle). https://www.houstonchronicle.com/news/investigations/abuse-of-faith/.

Earls, A. (Jan 30, 2023). *Public trust in pastors falls to historic low.* Lifeway Research. https://research.lifeway.com/2023/01/30/public-trust-in-pastors-falls-to-historic-low/#:~:text=As%20fewer%20Americans%20interact%20with,to%20the%20latest%20Gallup%20survey.

Egli, J. and D. Marable. (2014). *Small groups, big impact: Connecting people to God and one another in thriving groups.* CCS Pub.

Eswine, Z. (2015). *The imperfect pastor: discovering joy in our limitations through a daily apprenticeship with Jesus.* Crossway.

Gallaty, R. (2015). *Rediscovering discipleship: Making Jesus' final words our first work.* Zondervan.

Geiger, E. and K. Peck. (2016). *Designed to lead: The church and leadership development.* B&H Pub.

Gladen, S. (2013). *Leading small groups with purpose: Everything you need to lead a healthy group.* Baker Books.

Guelich, R. A. (1989). *Mark 1-8:26.* (Word Biblical Commentary). Zondervan Academic.

Hamilton, V. P. (2011). *Exodus: An exegetical commentary.* Baker Academic.

Hartwig, R. T., C. W. Davis, and J. A. Sniff. (2020). *Leading small groups that thrive: Five shifts to take your group to the next level.* Zondervan.

Jones, J. M. (June 26, 2023). *U.S. church attendance still lower than pre-pandemic.* Gallup. https://news.gallup.com/poll/507692/church-attendance-lower-pre-pandemic.aspx.

Kell, G. (Sep–Oct 2012). *Discipleship according to the scriptures.* 9 Marks Journal. https://www.9marks.org/article/journaldiscipleship-according-scriptures/.

Keller, T. (2002). *Why plant churches?.* https://download.redeemer.com/pdf/learn/resources/Why_Plant_Churches-Keller.pdf.

Kuo, L. (Jan 2019). *In China, they're closing churches, jailing pastors, –and even rewriting scripture.* https://www.theguardian.com/world/2019/jan/13/china-christians-religious-persecution-translation-bible.

Liederbach, M. (2017). *Chasing infinity: Discipleship as the pursuit of infinite treasure.* Cru Press.

Lifeway Research. (March 2022). *Pastoral burnout and loneliness.*

Luter, A. B. and N. Dodson. (2017). *Matured discipleship: Leadership in the synoptics and acts.* In B. K. Forrest and C. Roden (Eds.), *Biblical leadership: Theology for the everyday believer* (pp. 334–348).

Malphurs, A. and W. Mancini. (2004). *Building leaders: Blueprints for developing leadership at every level of your church.* Baker Books.

Mathews, K. A. (1996). *Genesis 1-11:26.* (NAC). Broadman & Holman.

Maxwell, J. C. (2007). *The 21 irrefutable laws of leadership.* HarperCollins Leadership.

Maxwell, J. C. (2012). *The 21 indispensable qualities of a leader*. Thomas Nelson.

McBride, N. (1990). *How to lead small groups*. NavPress.

Meyers, C.L. (2005). *Exodus*. (The New Cambridge Bible Commentary). Cambridge Press.

Nieuwhof, C. *Five shocking realities about the real state of pastor burnout*. https://careynieuwhof.com/5-shocking-realities-about-the-real-state-of-pastor-burnout/#:~:text=Barna%20CEO%20David%20Kinnaman%20recently,a%20-pastor%20or%20church%20leader.

Neill, S. (1959). *Creative tension*. (The Duff Lectures). Edinburgh House Press.

Perna, M. (2019). *Gen Z wants to change the world at your company*. Forbes. https://www.forbes.com/sites/markcperna/2019/12/10/gen-z-wants-to-change-the-world-at-your-company/?sh=1721f8523c56.

Peterson, E. (2011). *The pastor: A memoir*. Cited by https://www.youthworker.com/the-pastor-*eugene-peterson-on-how-to-be-an-unbusy-pastor*/#:~:text=%E2%80%9CWhy%20don't%20you%20let,Maybe%20we%20could%20learn.%E2%80%9D

Rainer, T. (2022). *10 things trending in the church for 2022*. Outreach Magazine. https://outreachmagazine.com/features/leadership/70027-10-things-trending-in-the-church-for-2022.html.

Rainer, T. (2023). *The great leadership shortage in churches*. Church Answers. https://churchanswers.com/blog/the-great-leadership-shortage-in-churches-five-ways-to-address-it/.

Rainer, T. (2024). *One key reason why church consultations fail*. Church Answers. https://churchanswers.com/blog/one-key-reason-why-church-consultations-fail/.

Roach, D. (Apr 2023). *1 in 4 pastors plan to retire by 2030*. Christianity Today. https://www.christianitytoday.com/news/2023/april/pastor-succession-church-next-generation-leader-barna-surve.html.

Sanchez, D. R. (2015). Strategies for starting churches. In J. M. Terry (Ed.), *Missiology: An introduction to the foundations, history, and strategies of world missions*. (Rev. ed) B&H Academic.

Sanders, J. O. (1989). *Spiritual leadership*. Moody Press.

Stetzer, E. and W. Bird. (2006). *The state of church planting in the United States: Research overview and qualitative study of primary church planting entities*. Christianity Today. www.christianitytoday.com/assets/10228.pdf.

Stetzer, E. and E. Geiger. (2014). *Transformational groups: Creating a new scorecard for groups*. B&H Publishing.

Strauss, M. L. (2017). *Mark*. (The Expositor's Bible Commentary). In T. Longman III and D. E. Garland (Eds.). Zondervan Academic. Kindle edition.

Stuart, D. K. (2006). *Exodus*. (NAC). Vol. 2. B&H.

Towns, E. L. (2014). *The ten most influential churches of the past century: And how they impact you today.* Destiny Image.

Tripp, P. D. (2012). *Dangerous calling: Confronting the unique challenges of pastoral ministry.* Crossway.

Scazzero, P. (2017). *Emotionally healthy spirituality: It's impossible to be spiritually mature while remaining emotionally immature.* Zondervan.

Wax, T. (2021). *On 'the rise and fall of mars hill'—surveying our souls.* https://www.thegospelcoalition.org/blogs/trevin-wax/rise-fall-mars-hill/.

Whitney, D. S. (2001). *Ten questions to diagnose your spiritual health.* NavPress.

www.ingramcontent.com/pod-product-compliance
Lightning Source LLC
Chambersburg PA
CBHW050646160426
43194CB00010B/1826